STUDIES IN BUSINESS ADMINISTRATION

Published under the Direction

of the

SCHOOL OF BUSINESS ADMINISTRATION
THE UNIVERSITY OF NORTH CAROLINA

Volume 1

LEADERSHIP FOR LIFE INSURANCE

LEADERSHIP FOR LIFE INSURANCE

The College Graduate in the Life Insurance Company Home Office

By OSCAR HARKAVY

Program in Economic Development
and Administration, The Ford Foundation
Formerly Research Associate, School of Business
Administration, University of North Carolina

Chapel Hill

PUBLISHED FOR THE SCHOOL OF BUSINESS ADMINISTRATION,
UNIVERSITY OF NORTH CAROLINA
BY THE UNIVERSITY OF NORTH CAROLINA PRESS

Manufactured in the United States of America

CMT

Van Rees Press • New York

✻ *Foreword* ✻

DURING the recent past, the School of Business Administration of the University of North Carolina at Chapel Hill has engaged in a cluster of research and training activities designed to assist business in the development of broad-gauged top management personnel. This study by Dr. Oscar Harkavy was made as part of the program.

In the academic year 1952-53, Dr. Willard J. Graham, under whose guidance the Executive Program at the University of Chicago was established, joined the faculty at Chapel Hill. In the fall of 1953 an Executive Program for senior management personnel of North Carolina and surrounding region was inaugurated at the University of North Carolina under his direction.

In December of 1952, the School of Business Administration organized and served as host to an international conference on executive development programs. Directors and teachers of such programs in thirteen universities in the United States and Canada were invited to participate in this conference, the aims of which were to clarify the objectives of executive development programs, to share experiences, and to point up policies of procedure for the benefit of the participating institutions.

Still another activity in the general area of executive development was carried out with a grant from the Committee for Economic Development. A group of business executives and School of Business Administration faculty members have cooperated in a study of executive development practices within North Carolina commerce and industry.

When the school was approached by the New York Life Insurance Company and asked how a grant in the field of life insurance might be used at Chapel Hill, it was natural to think in terms of management development. In modern business, a program of management development typically starts with the recruiting, selection, and training of college graduates. It seemed appropriate, therefore, to propose a study of this process as carried out by the life insurance industry. Inasmuch as considerable attention had been given to the recruitment and training of college-trained personnel for sales activities and relatively little or no parallel study for "home office" activities, it was decided to restrict the proposed study to the home office problem.

Dr. Dan McGill, now professor of insurance at the Wharton School of Finance and Commerce at the University of Pennsylvania and Executive Director of the S. S. Huebner Foundation for Insurance Education, was then Julian Price Associate Professor of Life Insurance at the University of North Carolina; he was on leave for service as an Air Force officer and was therefore unavailable for an indefinite period of time to engage in the proposed research activity. Accordingly, Dr. Oscar Harkavy, of the College of Business Administration at Syracuse University, was invited to join the faculty at Chapel Hill as a research associate for the purpose of carrying out this study. Dr. Harkavy is now a staff associate in the Program in Economic Development and Administration at The Ford Foundation.

The School of Business Administration at the University of North Carolina was honored to have been selected as one of the five institutions to which the New York Life Insurance Company awarded grants under its experimental program. The imaginative nature of this grant program reflects great credit upon both the company and the insurance industry, particularly upon Devereux C. Josephs, who was president of New York Life at the inception of the program and who is now its board chairman. It is our hope at the University of North Carolina that Dr. Harkavy's workmanlike volume will contribute to increased concern with the proper utilization of college-trained personnel by the life insurance industry and will thus justify the investment of a major portion of our New York Life Insurance Company grant to make possible the study and its publication.

Thomas H. Carroll
Dean

30 June 1954

* Preface *

THIS STUDY of the college graduate in the life insurance company home office may be of interest to life insurance company officers and employees, to college and university placement officials, to teachers of insurance, and to undergraduates who are casting about for a career. It is especially hoped that this study—or at least the Summary and Recommendations in Chapter Eight—will find its way to the attention of company top management, for without the enthusiastic sponsorship of the senior executives, a program of recruiting, training, and developing college graduates cannot be successful.

One of the most heartening experiences in this writer's lifetime has been the splendid cooperation given him in this research by literally hundreds of insurance company officers and employees, by dozens of college placement directors, and by a large number of recent college graduates. These people gave unstintingly of their time in submitting to interviews and in filling out lengthy questionnaires. Without their cooperation, this study could not have been made. Because the information has been provided on the condition that the informant remain anonymous, no individual is mentioned by name.

It is hoped that no confidences are broken by revealing in Appendix V the names of those insurance companies and educational institutions which contributed to the study. Some of the responding institutions replied anonymously and their contributions cannot be specifically acknowledged.

The writer is especially grateful to Dean Thomas H. Carroll of the School of Business Administration, University of North Carolina, who together with Mr. William O. Cummings, formerly Julian Price Lecturer in Life Insurance at the University of North Carolina and now consultant to the Life Insurance Agency Management Association, developed the original idea of this study and provided vital suggestions and encouragement throughout its execution. The writer is indebted to President William P. Worthington of the Home Life Insurance Company for suggesting that questionnaires be sent to recent college graduates who had refused positions with life insurance company home offices. He would also like to acknowledge his indebtedness to Mrs. Irene Garrett of the Business English Department and Professor William P. Gormbley, Director of Placement, College of Business Administration, Syracuse University; to Professor Dan M. McGill of the University of Pennsylvania; to Professor Frank J. Schwentker of the University of North Carolina; to Mr. Robert P. Stieglitz, Director of College Relations, the New York Life Insurance Company; and to Mr. Philip H. Yost, Personnel Assistant, the Connecticut General Life Insurance Company, for reading the manuscript and making many valuable suggestions. Any errors of fact and judgment remain, of course, the responsibility of the writer.

Finally, the writer wishes to acknowledge the hundreds of hours of editorial work and tabulation, as well as the many helpful suggestions, contributed by his wife, Frances Hoffman Harkavy, to whom this volume is affectionately dedicated.

Oscar Harkavy

❋ Contents ❋

III. AN APPRAISAL OF HOME OFFICE EMPLOYMENT OPPORTUNITIES

IV. RECRUITING COLLEGE GRADUATES

V. SELECTION

VI. TRAINING

VII. AFTER TRAINING

VIII. SUMMARY AND RECOMMENDATIONS

Appendices

✻ *Tables* ✻

TABLES

❋ *Introduction* ❋

✻ Introduction ✻

1. PURPOSE

THE purpose of this study is to examine the critical factors involved in the successful induction of young college graduates into one phase of the life insurance business. It is primarily concerned with non-selling, home office employment, rather than with sales positions. Widespread attention by experts has been given to the problem of utilizing young college graduates in sales. Therefore it was decided to avoid this question and to concentrate on home office employment.

This is no insignificant area of investigation. Nearly one-third of all those employed in the life insurance industry are home office personnel. At the end of 1951, 110,000 people—37,250 men and 72,750 women—worked in the home offices of the nation's more than 700 legal reserve life insurance companies. They are responsible for the management of the $73 billions of assets and the $276 billions of life insurance in force in these companies.[1]

2. SCOPE OF THE SURVEY

This study begins with a consideration of the life insurance industry's attitude toward the young college graduate. Do life insurance company officers welcome college graduates into their organizations? If so, are the companies getting a sufficient number, and are these of satisfactory caliber? What are the principal problems encountered by the companies in working with the new college graduate after he has been hired? In the second chapter, the point of view of the college graduate is taken up: What is his attitude toward a life insurance career? How successful

1. *Life Insurance Fact Book, 1953* (New York: Institute of Life Insurance, 1952), p. 10.

is the life insurance industry in competing with other branches of business for the new college graduate? What are the factors which make for its popularity or unpopularity? Chapter Three is devoted to an appraisal of home office employment opportunities by those in the best position to judge them: the company officers and employees themselves. The study continues, in Chapter Four, with a survey of techniques employed by life insurance companies for recruiting college graduates. It includes, in Chapter Five, an examination of the criteria and methods the companies use in selecting the individuals they want. Considerable attention is devoted in Chapter Six to the type of training made available to the graduate. Placement and management development activities are considered in Chapter Seven; after the college graduate completes his initial training period, what steps are undertaken to develop him so that eventually he will be ready for managerial responsibility?

The busy reader will find a summary of the report in Chapter Eight. This chapter also contains some recommendations which, it is hoped, will not be considered presumptuous on the part of an outsider.

3. SOURCES OF INFORMATION

a. *Life Insurance Companies*

In the course of this study, 65 life insurance companies were polled. Twenty-seven are mutual and 38 are stock companies. The writer visited 21 of these organizations during the summer of 1952 to obtain information from their officers. Data on the remaining 44 were gathered from responses to a detailed questionnaire distributed in September, 1952.[2] (See Appendix I, Questionnaire for Life Insurance Company Officers.) Although this sample of 65 out of nearly 700 legal reserve life insurance companies operating in the United States is not particularly large, it includes most of the largest companies. In fact, data were provided by 17 of the leading 20 companies in terms of asset size. Of the first 40 companies, 29 were visited or responded to questionnaires. As can be seen in Table 1, smaller organizations have not been excluded. Responses were obtained from 17 companies with assets under $50 million; 11 of the companies have less than 100 employees.

Organized college recruiting, training, and executive development activities are generally—but by no means exclusively—confined to the

2. Names of the companies were obtained from a comprehensive list and all responses were included in the sample.

larger companies, most of which are represented in this sample. Questionnaires were distributed to a large number of small companies. Many of these replied that the subject matter of the questionnaire is not relevant to their organization because of its small size. A large proportion of the small companies failed to return the questionnaire, while only a relatively small proportion of the very large companies failed to respond.

TABLE 1

Life Insurance Companies Sampled, Classified by Asset Size and by Number of Employees in Home Office

Asset Size	Number of Companies
Under $50 million	17
50-100 million	10
100-250 million	11
250-500 million	9
500-1,000 million	6
Over $1 billion	12
Total	65

Number of Employees in Home Office	Number of Companies
Under 100	11
100-250	13
250-500	14
500-1,000	9
1,000-5,000	12
Over 5,000	4
No information	2
Total	65

Source: Questionnaires sent to life insurance company officers (see Appendix I) and interviews.

Visits were confined to companies near the Eastern seaboard, but questionnaires were returned by companies located in all parts of the country. Table 2 shows the distribution of the companies polled by sections of the country.

The sample admittedly does not give proper representation to the great number of new companies which have recently been established, especially in the Southwest. (As of the end of 1951, Texas led the nation in the number of life insurance company home offices, with 138.) But it is probably a safe assumption that little formal activity of the kind surveyed in this report goes on in the small, newly organized company.

TABLE 2

LIFE INSURANCE COMPANIES SAMPLED, CLASSIFIED BY HOME OFFICE LOCATION

Region	Number of Companies
Northeast	23
Southeast	12
Midwest	17
Northwest	5
Southwest	8
Total	65

Source: Questionnaires sent to life insurance company officers (see Appendix I) and interviews.

b. *Placement Directors*

Information was also obtained from placement directors of 65 colleges and universities throughout the country. Visits with 9 academic officials were supplemented with questionnaire responses from 56 others. (See Appendix II, Questionnaire for College and University Placement Directors.) Fifty of these institutions offer degrees in business administration on the undergraduate or graduate level, as well as degrees in liberal arts. The remaining 15 do not grant business administration degrees, although some have a department of business administration within a college of liberal arts. As can be seen from Table 3, the greatest number of responses came from the Middle Atlantic and Midwest regions.

TABLE 3

COLLEGES AND UNIVERSITIES SAMPLED, CLASSIFIED BY LOCATION

Region	Number of Institutions
New England	8
Middle Atlantic	18
Southeast	9
Midwest	17
Northwest	3
Southwest	10
Total	65

Source: Questionnaires sent to college and university placement officers (see Appendix II) and interviews.

c. *College Graduates Who Rejected Life Insurance Employment*

In addition, a sample of 65[3] recent college graduates who rejected positions with life insurance companies was obtained by means of a questionnaire (see Appendix III). Thirty-eight of those responding are male, and 27 female. Of the males, 12 hold A.B. degrees, 22 have undergraduate degrees in business administration, and 2 are masters of business administration. All the females have A.B. degrees. Most of the individuals sampled were graduated in June, 1952. This sample cannot be considered representative of all recent college graduates since it contains only persons sufficiently interested in life insurance to make application to one or more life insurance companies.

Questionnaires were sent to recent graduates whose names and addresses appeared on lists provided by five companies. Each of these organizations has a highly developed program of college recruitment and training. An unsuccessful attempt was made to obtain similar lists from companies without such programs. The latter organizations either do not keep data on their college graduate job applicants or else had no applicants in this category in June, 1952.

d. *College-Level Employees*

During the summer of 1953, nine life insurance companies of different sizes in New York City, Newark, and Hartford were revisited in order that college graduates who had accepted employment in the home office might be interviewed. Information was obtained in private, confidential interviews with a total of 68 such individuals, including 63 men and 5 women. In each company, interviews were held with a cross-section of college-level employees in terms of length of service, occupation, and relative progress with the company.

The length of service of those interviewed, as indicated in Table 4, ranges from three months to 15 years, with decided concentration at the one- and two-year levels.

The employees occupy a wide assortment of positions. The three most frequently encountered areas of employment were underwriting, methods, and actuarial training. Fifty-nine of the employees are engaged in technical occupations, 7 in supervisory or administrative capacities, and 2 in non-technical, clerical, or secretarial positions.

3. It is pure coincidence that each sample contains 65 items.

TABLE 4

LENGTH OF SERVICE OF 68 COLLEGE-LEVEL LIFE INSURANCE COMPANY HOME OFFICE EMPLOYEES INTERVIEWED

Length of Service	Number
Less than 1 year	6
1 to 2 years	15
2 to 3 years	12
3 to 4 years	6
4 to 5 years	9
5 to 6 years	7
6 to 7 years	6
7 to 8 years	2
8 to 9 years	1
10 to 11 years	2
12 to 13 years	1
15 to 16 years	1
Total	68

Source: Interviews with college-level home office employees (see Appendix IV).

❋ The Life Insurance Company ❋ Looks At The College Graduate

Highlights of Chapter 1

An ever increasing proportion of new employees of life insurance company home offices is college-trained.

Home office positions for which life insurance companies most frequently recruit college graduates include: actuarial training, accounting, underwriting, security analysis, claims, and personnel.

While some company officials are dubious of the advisability of hiring many college graduates for home office work, most of the officers polled are satisfied with the adequacy of the graduates' college training, with their ability to get along with others, and with their attitude toward job responsibilities.

The most difficult problem in working with the college graduate is his desire to advance too rapidly.

Relations between non-college and college-trained personnel are generally reported to be good. Recently employed non-college personnel more readily accept the college-trained group than do older non-college employees.

Officers of a majority of smaller companies feel that they are currently obtaining as many college graduates as they can absorb; larger company officials are about evenly divided on this question.

Particularly in the larger companies, it is felt that the number of college graduates at present being obtained is insufficient to provide for the eventual replacement of junior and senior officers.

❋ *Chapter One* ❋

THE LIFE INSURANCE COMPANY LOOKS AT THE COLLEGE GRADUATE

THIS chapter considers the young college graduate through the eyes of the life insurance industry. It covers (1) the extent to which company officials and the rank and file of present employees are themselves college-trained; (2) the extent to which new employees are college-trained; (3) the positions for which new college graduates are recruited; (4) the attitude of company officers toward the employment of college graduates; (5) problems encountered as the result of the employment of college graduates; (6) the relations between the non-college employees and the college graduates; and finally (7) the opinion of company officers as to whether they are getting a sufficient number of new college graduates of satisfactory quality for their present and future needs.

1. COLLEGE GRADUATES IN THE HOME OFFICE

Do college graduates constitute a relatively large proportion of those employed by life insurance companies in their home offices?

A wide variation among companies is found. A much greater proportion of male than of female employees is college-trained. Most companies report that less than 5 per cent of their female employees—who constitute about two-thirds of all home office employees—have been graduated from college. On the other hand, the majority of companies polled indicated that somewhere between 10 and 50 per cent of their male employees went to college. Table 5 presents these data in greater detail.

The proportion of company officers who have graduated from college is considerably higher than that for all male employees. (Many com-

TABLE 5

PER CENT OF LIFE INSURANCE COMPANY HOME OFFICE EMPLOYEES COLLEGE-TRAINED

Female

Per Cent College Trained	*Number of Companies*
0- 5	19
5-10	8
Over 10	10
No information	28
Total	65

Male

Per Cent College Trained	*Number of Companies*
0- 10	5
10- 20	13
20- 50	14
50- 75	11
75-100	5
No information	17
Total	65

Source: Questionnaires sent to life insurance company officers (see Appendix I) and interviews.

panies have one or more female officers, but these are still considered something of a rarity.) Obviously, those who gained officer rank via the technical route—lawyers, physicians, and most actuaries—are college graduates. But many employees have reached high positions from beginnings as teen-aged mail clerks and office boys.

If the sample obtained from the questionnaire returns is representative of the industry as a whole, a greater proportion of senior officers [1] than of junior officers has attended college. This conclusion can be reached from Table 6.

There is, of course, considerable variation from company to company. No significant association was found between the proportion of officers having college training and the size or location of the company.

The extent to which a given company's officer personnel is college-trained undoubtedly conditions its enthusiasm for the recruitment of

1. "Senior" was defined in the questionnaire as department head and above.

new college graduates. There are companies, one is told, in which the senior officers did not have a college education and are proud of the fact that they are "self-made" men. In the belief that others can follow in their footsteps, they make little effort to acquire college-educated employees except for certain technical positions. On the other hand, there are several outstanding examples of companies headed by non-college people who are particularly eager to employ a large percentage of college graduates. These executives are anxious for young people to take advantage of the college experience which they themselves missed. In general, however, a favorable attitude toward the new college graduate is more prevalent in companies with a substantial proportion of college-trained senior officers.

TABLE 6

PROPORTION OF LIFE INSURANCE COMPANY SENIOR AND JUNIOR OFFICERS WITH COLLEGE TRAINING

Per Cent College Trained	Per Cent of Companies*	
	Senior Officers	*Junior Officers*
0- 10	0	9
10- 25	3	4
25- 50	12	26
50- 75	39	31
75- 90	37	15
90-100	9	15
Total	100	100

* Based on a sample of 43 companies.

Source: Questionnaires sent to life insurance company officers (see Appendix I) and interviews.

2. RECENT TRENDS IN HOME OFFICE EMPLOYMENT

During recent years many companies report that a large proportion of their newly hired male employees has been college-trained. Some companies indicate that with the exception of employees hired for building maintenance, printing, and other such skilled and semi-skilled occupations, virtually all of their new male employees have received a college education. An executive of one company reports that his organization has had more college recruits in the past 5 years than in the preceding 50 years. Another reports that he hires only one non-college male employee for every 50 college graduates. On the other hand, those companies responding to the questionnaire present a rather varied pattern, as can be seen in Table 7:

TABLE 7

PER CENT OF NEW MALE EMPLOYEES COLLEGE-TRAINED, 1947-1952*

Per Cent College-Trained	Number of Companies
0- 10	8
10- 25	5
25- 50	11
50- 75	2
75- 90	8
90-100	3
No information	28
Total	65

* Excluding employees hired for printing, building maintenance, etc., as well as legal and medical positions.

Source: Questionnaires sent to life insurance company officers (see Appendix I) and interviews.

While some organizations have established programs for recruiting college women, most females continue to be hired for clerical positions which do not require a college degree.

One obvious reason for the increase in the proportion of college graduates hired by insurance companies is the fact that there are more college graduates in the labor force as a whole than there were before World War II. But more significant is the opinion expressed by many executives that the bright high school graduate will find a way of getting a higher education, even if his family cannot finance him. He can take advantage of the educational benefits of the "G.I. Bill", of privately endowed scholarships, and of low-tuition state and municipal colleges.[2] These executives feel, therefore, that the high school graduate who does not avail himself of such an opportunity for further education is likely to lack the intelligence and ambition necessary to rise above the minor clerical positions. They are quick to point out, on the other hand, that these opportunities were not so readily available for employees hired during the depression of the thirties and earlier, and that many among this group possess the leadership potential which they ascribe to today's

2. On the other hand, the President's Commission on Higher Education reports that only half of the students who rank in the top quarter of their high school graduating classes attend college.

college graduate. A top executive of one large company indicated, for example, that a company must bring in some college graduates today to get the same average "I.Q." obtainable from a group of high school graduates of fifteen or twenty years ago.

Another reason for the large percentage of college graduates among new male recruits is the fact that personnel people are finding it increasingly difficult to attract the high school graduate to a white collar, clerical position, since he can generally enjoy a higher starting wage in a "blue collar" job in industry.

3. POSITIONS FOR WHICH NEW COLLEGE GRADUATES ARE RECRUITED

What are the positions for which life insurance companies customarily recruit new college graduates? Company personnel officers were asked this question, and the number of times each position was mentioned is tabulated in Table 8.

TABLE 8

HOME OFFICE POSITIONS FOR WHICH LIFE INSURANCE COMPANIES CUSTOMARILY RECRUIT NEW COLLEGE GRADUATES

Position	Number of Times Mentioned
Actuarial training	47
Accounting	35
Underwriting	30
Security analysis	29
Claims	19
Personnel	19
Mortgage analysis	17
Statistics	16
Methods	14
Group policyholder service	14
Advertising	12

Others mentioned include: Administrative training, office management, sales promotion, library supervision, benefit analysis, clerical supervision, group administration, cost allocation, group contract drafting, secretarial, clerical, research.

Source: Questionnaires sent to life insurance company officers (see Appendix I).

This list excludes physicians and lawyers. Some companies make the practice of recruiting these professionals right out of law school and internship, but a far greater number of personnel officials indicated that they generally hire physicians and lawyers after they have engaged in outside practice for a period of years.

Young college graduates generally prefer staff to line positions. The officer in charge of college recruiting for a large, multiple-line company offering a wide range of positions finds many enthusiastic candidates for a small number of openings in publicity work. When asked what home office positions are most popular with their graduates, placement officers tended to mention such functions as personnel, accounting, costs, methods, procedures, and statistical work. Several mentioned claims adjusting work, but one may suspect they had property and casualty insurance in mind. Only one placement officer included underwriting among the popular positions. On the other hand, five specifically mentioned underwriting as among the least attractive positions. As one placement officer put it, "specific positions which seem to be 'dead-end', such as underwriting and clerical" do not arouse enthusiam among their graduates. One of the most successful college recruiters makes it a practice to stress the more glamorous staff positions when explaining employment opportunities to groups of undergraduates. He emphasizes the availability of such positions as economic and market research, advertising, sales promotion, publications, cost allocation and budgetary control, personnel, and methods.

An actuarial officer who has occasion to interview large numbers of female college graduates noted that most of the girls with whom he talks seek staff positions, particularly in personnel. On one occasion he told a young lady that his company employs 5,000 people in the home office in addition to 7,000 in the field and asked her to estimate the number of individuals employed in the personnel department. Her estimate: "About 2,000." Actually, this department has about 60 people, most of whom occupy clerical positions. Only 17 of the 60 are college-trained.

Some companies have hired college graduates for routine work as a short-term remedy for the shortage of clerical help, since in some areas it is easier to obtain college than high school graduates. The company officer who pointed this out declared that he considers this practice fair neither to the college graduate, whose talents are not being properly used, nor to the high school graduate, who usually gets lower pay for performing the same function.

Included among "other positions mentioned" in Table 8 is that of "administrative training." Only two respondents to the questionnaire mentioned it. There are several other companies which hire for an administrative training program rather than for a specific position. It is noteworthy that 51 of the placement officers polled feel that their students show a strong preference for companies offering a formal training program, while only 3 do not. The question of the formal training program will be considered in Chapter Six.

4. COMPANY ATTITUDE TOWARD THE EMPLOYMENT OF NEW COLLEGE GRADUATES

Company executives are by no means unanimous in their desire to hire an ever increasing proportion of college graduates. For example, one president made a survey of the personnel of his organization and came to the conclusion that high school graduates had been more successful than the college graduates in his company. "There are many positions," he states, "in which practical apprenticeship in some of the more mundane aspects of the business is highly desirable. One objection that college graduates have to insurance is that they must devote themselves for so long to a vast amount of monotonous detail before advancement to another position. . . . With the development of the L.O.M.A. movement and the other educational activities going on in the business, . . . more and more it will be possible for the business to provide within its own walls the higher education necessary to fit a man for the higher ranks. . . ."[3]

The vice-president of a small company expressed himself in positive terms in a letter to the author:

> It has been our experience in the past that the average male college graduate comes to our organization with the feeling of "How long will it take him to be President of the Company?" "What are the retirement plans for the employees?" "What job fringe benefits will be given him?" He totally lacks the understanding that his next forty years with the Company are important to him. We feel instead of retirement, he should be looking to the present and the immediate future. Too many graduates are too interested in the future instead of the present, and after all, unless a Company can get some economic value out of a man in the present, it will have no profits to give him in the future.

Even those who are convinced of the value of higher education realize the dangers of overhiring college graduates. The Personnel Director of a company which is recognized as a leader in the recruitment and training of college graduates for home office positions cautions against

3. "Case of the High School and College Graduate," *The National Underwriter* (April 28, 1950), p. 10.

excessive recruiting of college men lest too many men compete for a limited number of upper-level jobs, with a disastrous effect on morale.

All in all, however, officers of companies that have had experience working with new college graduates are generally pleased with their performance in terms of the adequacy of their training, their ability to get along with others, and their attitude toward job responsibilities. While recent graduates who are veterans of military service are naturally found somewhat more mature and serious-minded than non-veterans, few of the companies note significant differences in their respective abilities.

a. *Adequacy of College Training*

Officers of only 2 of the 65 companies polled declared flatly that they consider that the academic training received by college graduates they hire is inadequate. A majority of the respondents found no particular deficiencies in the graduates' training, although a substantial minority pointed out specific shortcomings. They are most frequently critical of the young college graduate's ability in English and in mathematics. Said one personnel officer: "College graduates are woefully weak in their ability to write and speak English. Their language is limited and filled with clichés." Several officers of large Eastern companies feel that more attention should be given to the humanities and other liberal arts areas, especially by those who concentrate in business administration. Other officers, however, find fault with the lack of specific preparation in business subjects on the part of candidates for employment with their companies. Life insurance principles, accounting, and business machine procedures were cited as areas of deficiency. Another believes the colleges offer "too little training in pre-Keynesian economics." Certain training officers criticized their graduates' training in more general terms. Several feel that the typical college man is too reluctant to think for himself, that he wants "a rule book outlining a step-by-step procedure for everything." A criticism along the same lines was voiced by one questionnaire respondent who noted: "Training has been in terms of 'textbook' and abstraction. Experience with and recognition of practical situations is too limited."

Recent college graduates currently employed in home offices were asked to comment on deficiencies in their college training. Many of them would like to have taken specific technical courses in the area in which they are working. Few had any idea they would enter the insurance business upon graduation, and none, except for the actuarial students, knew what specific function they would find themselves performing. Thus a speech major now in personnel work wishes he had studied more psychology and industrial relations, and a pre-medical student engaged in mortgage underwriting wishes he had taken some work in real estate. Many such people plan to fill in specific deficiencies with additional night courses.

Perhaps the most important general deficiency mentioned is in mathematics. Eleven of the 68 interviewed wish they had studied more mathematics. Many of the home office positions, even those outside the actuarial department, require some mathematical facility. Other areas of deficiency mentioned include accounting and economics (especially by liberal arts graduates) and English composition (especially by engineering and business administration graduates). A substantial number in the interviewed group feel they would have been helped by a survey course in life insurance prior to employment. An actuarial student who was a mathematics major in a liberal arts college claimed that it takes about a year of employment to become familiar with insurance terminology without previous college work in insurance.

One man believes that he devoted himself too exclusively to his studies while in college. Had he entered more extra-curricular activities, he would, he feels, be able to meet people more easily in his present position.

b. *Ability to Get Along with Others*

In comments on the ability of young college graduates to get along with others, only one company officer flatly declared this to be "poor." Another noted that college recruits show "some tendency to overestimate their own capabilities without experience, which tends to be annoying to established employees." All the others, however, made favorable remarks ranging from "satisfactory" to "excellent."

Company officials stressed the importance of careful screening and proper orientation in producing satisfactory relations between college and non-college graduates. These officials try to select only those who are likely to mix easily with people of all backgrounds. In the course of orientation, the college people are cautioned not to set themselves apart from the rest of the employees, nor to give undue publicity to the "old school tie." "After all," said one executive, "having a college degree is no longer exciting."

c. *Attitude toward Job Responsibilities*

The attitude toward job responsibilities taken by the typical college graduate is considered quite satisfactory by the overwhelming majority of the companies polled. Only one response of "poor" was obtained, and this from the same officer who was most critical in his comments on college training and the ability of graduates to get along with others. Two other officers reported this attitude to be only "fair," and another indicated that his answer of "satisfactory" was actually "damning with faint praise." This officer remarked: "They take about as much training as the non-college group."

Most officers were kinder to the graduates. The following comments are typical:

"They generally try very hard."

"Normally ready to accept responsibility when given the opportunity."

"Better than the non-graduate."

"Accepts and discharges responsibilities to the best of his understanding."

The routine nature of many of the lower-level insurance company positions is well known, and several officers noted impatience with this routine on the part of many college graduates. But it is generally agreed that if the individual feels "it won't last forever," he is willing to undergo a considerable amount of clerical routine.

The adverse comment made most frequently is that the young college-trained employee often wishes to move forward to new positions of greater responsibility more rapidly than his superiors feel that he can. One officer describes this tendency thus: "Usually they are eager and do accept responsibilities. Occasionally they want more than they are capable of handling." And another: "They are somewhat lacking in appreciation that responsibilities are earned, not given."

d. *Problems in Working with Young College Graduates*

The problem encountered most often in working with the college graduate after he has been selected and hired has been mentioned in the section immediately above: it is his desire to progress too rapidly. This was expressed by an anonymous company president who wrote:

> Today many of the college graduates are discontented. They want to move along more rapidly than the insurance structure will allow. Their income is

not increasing rapidly enough to suit them and their desire is to assume positions of increased responsibility faster than they are ready for them or more rapidly than these positions become available.[4]

Company officials were asked to comment on this statement in the light of their own companies' experience. Forty-seven out of 58 replying to this question expressed their agreement; only 11 disagreed. Several officers suggested reasons for this discontent in addition to the natural restlessness of youth. Veterans are impatient to make up for the time lost in military service. Those with families are anxious to get them out of a flat and into a home of their own. This is particularly true of college graduates, since a majority come from families of relatively high economic status. They wish to enjoy as soon as possible the same standard of living as their parents.

Some companies have avoided this problem by means of their employee selection policy. They limit the number of new people hired in order that most of them will have favorable opportunities for advancement. (One personnel officer noted, too, that the extremely ambitious person who would be contented with nothing less than a meteoric rise to the top would not seek home office employment in the first place.) Nor is the problem acute for companies that have experienced rapid growth. One officer writes: "Opportunity for advancement is often available before the college graduate is ready to assume increased responsibility."

The problem is by no means limited to the life insurance home office. One placement director observed that graduates often write to her to complain that they have worked six months without a promotion. The Director of Placement at Northwestern University reports that officers in 44 out of 100 companies in all branches of industry criticize the desire for too rapid promotion on the part of young college graduates.[5]

It might be assumed that this over-eagerness for promotion results in a greater turnover of college-trained than of non-college personnel. This, however, is not the case. The companies responding to the questionnaire were asked to compare turnover among college graduates with that among non-college *male* employees. (Female employees were excluded because the extremely high turnover of female clerical help

4. *Ibid.*

5. Frank S. Endicott, "Trends in Employment of College and University Graduates in Business and Industry," *School and College Placement,* XI (Mar. 1951), 54.

would make meaningless a comparison with all non-college employees.) Out of 45 companies providing this information, 9 reported that college graduate turnover is greater, 16 reported that it is about the same, and 20 reported that it is lower. If this sample is representative, the college graduate does not present a special turnover problem.

Two of the respondents who noted other problems commented on the difficulty of making the transition between the classroom and the business world. The difficulty, according to one reply, is that of "learning the difference between theory and practice." The other remarked that it is "hard for some to adjust from the idealistic touch of the classroom to the realistic view of the business world." A problem singled out for mention by two respondents is a failure to give sufficient attention to the details involved in administration of the life insurance business. Two others found their college-trained employees insufficiently willing to work or to take the training program seriously enough.

5. ATTITUDES OF NON-COLLEGE EMPLOYEES TOWARDS NEW COLLEGE GRADUATES

Company officers were asked how they would characterize the attitude toward new college graduates on the part of non-college-trained employees. On the supposition that there is a difference between the attitude of recent employees and those of several years' service, the respondents were asked to comment on each group separately. About 60 per cent reported that recently employed non-college personnel take a friendly attitude; about one-third reported a neutral attitude; and the remaining 6 per cent indicated some hostility toward the graduates. The older employees were reported to be somewhat less cordial in their relations with the new college graduates, although slightly more than half the companies reported that friendly relations obtain. About 22 per cent of the respondents noted significant antagonism on the part of this group, and one-fourth reported a neutral attitude. The difference between the older and younger groups is evident from the responses of individual companies to this query. Where recent employees are considered "friendly," the older employees are merely "tolerant." In a company where the recent employees' attitude toward the graduates is characterized as "indifferent," some resentment is found on the part of the older personnel.

In many respects this question depends upon the new graduate's ability to get along with others. As one respondent wrote: "Certainly no resentment unless college graduate assumes a superior attitude and then the resentment is terrific."

Some jealousy toward female college graduates was reported. On the other hand, personnel officers pointed out that few female non-college employees plan to make a career in insurance and hence are less likely to care whether or not college graduates threaten their advancement with the company.

Among the older employees, some respondents noted "jealousy and fear for the future," a feeling that "college graduates are paid too much and progress too rapidly," or a tendency to regard experience as more important than education. But other officials find this group making "a genuine effort to be helpful," showing "occasional mild resentment," but "a generally favorable attitude." One writes:

> Recent employees and those with several years of service are informed about the purpose and need for college-trained personnel. They know that performance determines opportunities. Growth of company requires additional personnel and college trainees will not supplant them but augment them.

The college-level employees interviewed were asked about their relations with non-college personnel. While about one-third noted some resentment on the part of fellow employees without college background, no one interviewed regarded this as a major problem.

In a considerable number of instances, the recent college graduate finds himself in a section composed almost exclusively of people with similar background. This situation was reported by people in such areas as group service and group underwriting, investment analysis, expense analysis, and agency supervision. These people are isolated from the rank and file of non-college employees and naturally have no first-hand experience of resentment on the part of other employees.

A majority of those interviewed, however, work side by side with non-college people and report that friendly relations obtain. They realize that there are several factors which naturally cause resentment. Young college graduates are employed at starting salaries which are not very much lower than those made by non-college people with long periods of service with the company. In organizations where emphasis is placed on recruiting and training college-level employees, the non-college people feel that they are being discriminated against. A lunch companion of one college man used to complain: "I've been here 25 years and have never been late once. It never even got me a seat in the park." College people are frequently singled out for special assignments within a section, while the others are left with the clerical routine. In one instance, a new division was set up in an old line department and was manned entirely by college graduates. It was separated from the rest of the department by a half partition and furnished with brand new desks and equipment, in contrast to the older furniture used by the rest of the department. This symbolized the favored position of the college graduate and caused considerable resentment on the part of the other employees.

But those who noted these sources of resentment reported that it was seldom directed against them as individuals. Many indicated that they make a special effort to get along with non-college people and usually succeed. They are careful that nothing in their actions or manner will give rise to resentment, and make it a point to request the advice and help of their non-college colleagues as often as possible.

One college graduate who has been employed in the home office for seven years was hired at $3000 per year, which he believes was greater than half the male employees in the company were making at the time. The attitude of the older employees toward him was: "Who the heck is he to be making so much?" As time went on and he got to know his fellow employees as individuals, this resentment disappeared. Now he finds himself resenting brand new college graduates coming into the company at substantial salaries. He finds this to be a natural human attitude, irrelevant to the question of college versus non-college employees.

Only three of the 68 graduates interviewed noted resentment toward college graduates on the part of supervisory personnel. Of course, in many cases, particularly in the more technical operations, most of the supervisors are themselves college graduates. But others reported a most favorable reception by non-college supervisors. One man noted that when he was first employed, lower-level supervisors had the "usual attitude toward impractical college training"; but when he showed them that "he could do a day's work," their hostility wore off. Another found that many of these individuals go out of their way to be friendly and helpful, even though they resent the apparently favored position of the college graduate.

Not a few officials of companies which do not offer an organized college training program declared that, while non-college employee attitude is satisfactory at present, if a special program were to be established for college graduates and if a large number of the latter were to be brought into the company at once, there would be much resentment. In fact, this is one of the chief reasons given for the failure to institute such programs. Companies which do have special college programs generally find such fears unfounded. This problem is discussed at greater length in Chapter Six, in connection with the placement of training program graduates.

6. SUCCESS IN MEETING REQUIREMENTS FOR NEW COLLEGE GRADUATES

a. *Immediate Requirements*

Despite criticism of the new college graduates' shortcomings, most companies look to this group to fill an important manpower requirement. Are companies obtaining a sufficient number of new college graduates for their present needs?

Of the 60 organizations whose officers answered this question, 39 were reported to be getting a sufficient number for their immediate needs in 1952; 21 were said to be getting an inadequate number. A majority of the smaller companies were satisfied with the number of graduates they hired, but the larger companies are about evenly divided in their opinion. This is understandable, since the smaller companies' needs are more modest and hence more easily filled.

Life insurance companies can be roughly divided into two classifications: a small minority which has established organized college recruiting programs to fill pre-determined annual quotas; and the majority, which hires an occasional college man as a vacancy arises. About half the companies in the first group obtained a sufficient number as of 1952. Some of the companies with organized recruiting programs indicated that, although they were successful in filling quotas prior to 1952, in that year they had difficulty, due primarily to the draft and to the increasingly higher salaries offered by other industries competing for college graduates. Despite the absence of an organized recruiting program, a majority of the companies in the second group reported that they obtained a sufficient number of college graduates in 1952. One should conclude, not that organized college recruiting hinders the acquisition of college graduates, but rather that the companies without such programs are less convinced of the need for substantial numbers of college trained personnel, and their requirements are therefore more readily satisfied.

b. *Future Requirements*

When the company officers were asked if they are obtaining a sufficient number of new college graduates for their future needs, specifically for the eventual replacement of junior and senior officers, 31 of the companies replying to the questionnaires indicated that they are; 29 reported that they are not. Again, while most of the smallest companies do not recognize an officer replacement problem, all the largest companies (those with assets exceeding $1 billion) state that they are not obtaining a sufficient number for their future needs.

A top executive of a giant company declared: "Insurance companies are lagging behind industry in general in their recruiting of college-trained personnel. In the future, key positions will more and more be occupied by college people." Another officer echoed the opinion of many in the industry when he said: "If we don't recruit college men, we shall have to hire people for top level jobs from other companies. This is certainly more destructive of morale than bringing in college men in training positions." The president of a small company finds his major problem is the development of second echelon management. At present he must go outside the company for such people; there he finds a tight competitive market for good actuaries, insurance accountants, underwriters, and claims men. He would much rather develop candidates for such positions within the company, and this entails college recruiting on a larger scale than heretofore.

A troublesome dilemma is apparent. On the one hand many companies maintain that they cannot absorb more college-trained employees at the moment, while on the other hand they foresee difficulties in finding officer replacements in the future unless they continually bring in new college graduates at the trainee level.

The training director of one company stated, for example, that the development of formal management replacement charts would force the adoption of an organized college recruitment program. But the vice-president in charge of personnel in this same company felt that his organization was obtaining all the new college graduates it could absorb at the moment. A senior executive of another large company which has no formal recruiting program felt that this policy may be "double-crossing the top management of twenty-five years from now" in not providing college-trained supervisory and management material at this time. The vice-president of a small southern company also believes he is obtaining a sufficient number of college graduates for his present needs, recognizing at the same time a shortage of junior men who will be available to replace senior officers. As is the case in many companies, a large number of his organization's junior officers, having attained their rank through long years of service with the company, are near retirement age themselves and thus will be unable to assume executive positions.

* *The College Graduate Looks at the Life Insurance Company* *

Highlights of Chapter 2

Most college and university placement officers believe that the life insurance industry is not getting its share of top-notch graduates because: (1) knowledge of the life insurance industry on the part of college students is inaccurate or inadequate; (2) to most college students, a life insurance career means sales on commission; (3) starting salaries are below those offered by industrial firms; (4) home office positions are considered to involve too much clerical routine.

The principal critical factors causing the college graduates polled to refuse home office employment include: (1) low starting salary, (2) uncertain opportunities for advancement in salary and responsibility, (3) uninteresting work.

Except for actuarial trainees, few college graduates consciously prepare for an insurance career while undergraduates. Most of those interviewed who had accepted insurance employment were recruited on campus, have relatives in the business, or "just stumbled" upon home office employment.

* Chapter Two *

THE COLLEGE GRADUATE LOOKS AT THE LIFE INSURANCE COMPANY

During the past few years, keen competition for the services of new college graduates by the nation's leading business firms has created an abnormal employment situation. Each of the more prominent colleges and universities receives recruiting representatives from literally hundreds of corporations. An able graduate usually has employment offers from half a dozen leading firms at salaries which often exceed those earned by his professors. How successful is the life insurance industry in competing for its share of the top-notch graduates in this unusual employment market?

Chapter Two presents a view of life insurance company home office employment opportunities through the eyes of college and university placement officers and of a group of the graduates themselves. The survey of placement officers gives their answers to such questions as: (1) Do life insurance companies obtain their fair share of top-notch college graduates? (2) How popular is a life insurance career and what are the reasons for its popularity or lack of popularity? (3) How does life insurance company home office employment compare in popularity with other phases of insurance work? The survey of recent graduates who have rejected offers of employment in life insurance company home offices is an attempt to discover the critical factors which caused them to refuse such employment. Finally, the circumstances are examined under which the group of college-level home office employees interviewed happened to take insurance company positions.

The student attitudes reported in this chapter are seldom based on widespread knowledge of actual conditions in the life insurance industry. As a matter of fact, it will be pointed out that students are either uninformed or else misinformed about the opportunities offered in life insurance. Nonetheless, these students are governed in their employment decisions by the attitudes described in this chapter and, justified or not, these attitudes determine the success or failure of the recruiting efforts of life insurance companies.

1. THE LIFE INSURANCE COMPANY'S SHARE OF TOP-NOTCH COLLEGE GRADUATES [1]

College and university placement officers were asked whether they believe life insurance companies are getting their share of top-notch graduates. Forty-eight replied in the negative, only 13 in the affirmative. When asked if there are specific companies which do obtain their share, a majority answered "yes." Just a few supplied the names of the successful ones. One very large company was mentioned seven times, a somewhat smaller one six times, a medium-sized company four times, and another very large organization three times. Other companies mentioned either are exclusively property and casualty companies—although the question specified life insurance companies—or write these lines in addition to life. In interviews with other placement officers in Eastern and Southern schools, the same four or five names were continually mentioned.

It is significant that college and university placement officers located in all parts of the country mention only a handful of companies as getting their share of top-notch graduates. These companies stand out from the rest in several characteristics: (1) they employ a professional college recruiting staff whose members are highly regarded by placement people; this staff, in the case of most of the companies mentioned, operates out of the home office, rather than from branch offices or agencies; (2) they have a rather elaborate selection process which involves a visit to the home office by selected candidates at company expense; (3) they have established a formal training program; (4) they take pains in the proper placement of the graduates after their training. Much of the detailed information on recruiting, selection, and training contained in succeeding chapters was obtained from this small group of companies.

1. See the pioneer study in insurance company recruiting: H. G. Kenegy and Others, *Getting Our Share of the Annual College Crop* (Hartford: Life Insurance Agency Management Association, 1949).

2. POPULARITY OF THE LIFE INSURANCE INDUSTRY COMPARED WITH THAT OF OTHER INDUSTRIES COMPETING FOR THE COLLEGE GRADUATE

Insurance is by no means a glamorous industry in the eyes of today's college graduate. Those industries which have captured the young man's imagination are the growing manufacturing industries, such as oils, chemicals, machinery, and electronics. For college women the "glamor" jobs are in advertising, radio and publishing. Placement officers were asked how the life insurance industry ranks in popularity with other industries bidding for their graduates. Of those replying, 43 ranked it as "below average," 9 as "average," one as "above average," and one as "very popular." At a large metropolitan university, the placement director indicated that in six and a half years on the job he has never had an unsolicited inquiry about opportunities in life insurance company home offices. Other officers interviewed, however, have found some interest in actuarial work among mathematics majors and also some interest in non-actuarial home office employment on the part of students with family connections in insurance. Several placement officials asserted that it is often necessary to pressure students into agreeing to be interviewed by insurance representatives by refusing to allow them interviews with companies they are anxious to join unless they take some insurance interviews too. An officer of a southern university cited the example of a boy who was "infuriated" when asked to interview an insurance company representative when he was under consideration by Armstrong Cork, Shell Oil, and Eastman Kodak. It happened that he accepted employment with an insurance company and is at present in a better position than many of his classmates who took industrial employment. A survey of Harvard seniors in 1950-1951 [2] indicates that only 8 out of 359 students desiring non-professional employment were considering any phase of insurance. More popular than insurance is manufacturing and production, in which 98 planned to seek employment; next came government service with 55, marketing with 38, writing and journalism with 26, advertising and public relations with 23, personnel and industrial relations with 18, investments with 14, and banking with 9. The 8 looking to insurance as a career are an even smaller fraction of the total graduating class than these

2. Donald S. Bradshaw and Alexander Clark, *Occupational Plans of Harvard Seniors, 1950-1951* (Cambridge, Massachusetts: Office of Student Placement, Harvard University, 1951), p. 8.

figures would indicate, since 52 per cent of the class planned to enter the professions, and were therefore excluded from this tabulation.

One might expect the situation to be different in colleges of business administration, where almost the entire graduating class anticipates a career in business. But placement officers point out that insurance recruiters may evoke more response at a liberal arts college than at a business administration school. This is because the business administration student generally seeks employment in his major field of concentration. On the other hand, liberal arts graduates, who are less likely to have built up strong preferences for any particular field of business, appear more willing to examine the opportunities offered in insurance with an open mind. A placement officer reports that, while the school of business administration of his university has the nation's outstanding insurance faculty, nonetheless other areas of concentration, particularly those connected with industrial management, have much more student appeal. At the business administration college with which the writer is connected, the proportion of the student body majoring in insurance has not exceeded 3 per cent in the past seven years.

What are the reasons for the relative unpopularity of the insurance industry with college students?

The characteristic response of placement officers to this question is that, to most undergraduates, life insurance employment means life insurance sales on commission. They are unaware of non-sales opportunities with life companies, and hence shy away from insurance because selling an intangible on commission is one of the least popular careers in the eyes of most college students. They want the security of a salary, at least for the first few years. New college graduates lack sufficient self-assurance to plunge into commission selling. They dislike the idea of selling policies to their friends. Poorly selected and trained agents whom they have encountered have left them with a bad impression of the insurance business as a whole. One placement officer refers to a "local overabundance of over-eager, not too tactful, door-to-door insurance salesmen." The placement officers interviewed stated that knowledge of the industry is poor, and their colleagues throughout the country who were polled generally agree on this point. When asked how they would appraise the average student's knowledge of the life insurance industry and home office employment opportunities, 43 replied that they consider it to be "poor," 8 believe it to be "average," and 3 think it "excellent."

In schools where courses in insurance are offered, somewhat better knowledge of these employment opportunities is reported. Where an insurance major is offered, knowledge of the business appears somewhat better still. Nonetheless, placement officers of 13 out of 19 schools offering a major in insurance reported poor knowledge of insurance opportunities on the part of the student. This is not surprising, in view of the limited number of insurance majors on most campuses. Furthermore, typical college courses in insurance, even those exclusively devoted to life insurance, seldom give much attention to home office activities. When the college student is made aware of home office employment opportunities, as distinct from sales, he frequently becomes more enthusiastic about a career in insurance. His enthusiasm may be dampened, however, by the relatively low starting salaries offered by most life insurance companies.

There is some divergence of experience among the placement officers, but they generally agree that public accounting, industrial accounting, tangible sales, and production management positions commanded higher starting salaries in 1952 than did home office positions in life insurance companies. On the other hand, starting salaries in banking, intangible sales, retailing, and utilities are considered to be about equal to those in life insurance, and there is no agreement at all on the relative position of advertising. Table 9 recapitulates the responses of the placement officers on the competitive position of life insurance company starting salaries.

While placement officers report that intelligent college students will often take positions with low starting salaries when they feel the long-range opportunities are exceptional, life companies cannot compete with other branches of business if their salaries are too far out of line. One placement director pointed out that pride is involved in accepting a starting salary. A student will hesitate to accept $50 a week when his friends are starting at $300 a month. In recent years, many new graduates already have family responsibilities. In their cases an adequate starting salary is a matter of necessity rather than of pride alone.

Low starting salary is not the only reason for the relative unpopularity of insurance work. According to placement officers, college students feel home office positions lack glamor; too much of the job involves clerical routine. They believe that advancement is slow in the home office, except for those specially trained in law, medicine, or mathematics. One placement director feels the life insurance companies must engage more vigorously than they have in executive development programs in order to attract the able and ambitious college graduate. The location of home offices was cited as a deterrent by some placement people, particularly in the South. Many students are averse to leaving their native state for the insurance centers of New England, New York, or Philadelphia.

TABLE 9

Starting Salaries Offered to Non-Technical College Graduates by Life Insurance Companies for Home Office Positions, Compared with Starting Salaries in Other Areas of Employment, 1952

	Number of Schools Reporting		
	Above Life Insurance	*Equal to Life Insurance*	*Below Life Insurance*
Accounting, public	26	14	5
Accounting, industrial	34	9	1
Advertising	12	12	20
Banking	5	16	25
Sales, tangible	37	7	2
Sales, intangible	16	24	2
Production management	42	6	0
Retailing	5	25	17
Utilities	15	24	3

Source: Questionnaires sent to college and university placement officers (see Appendix II).

Several placement directors indicated that the response life insurance company recruiters evoke on their campuses is closely related to the enthusiasm with which the student body has accepted the insurance courses offered. In some institutions a particularly popular insurance professor has been instrumental in encouraging an unusual number of applicants for insurance employment. Therefore the placement officers were asked to rate their school's insurance program in terms of student body enthusiasm. Of 46 officers responding, only 2 rated it as "outstanding," and 8 as "above average." Eighteen rated it as "average" and another 18 as "below average." Obviously, the insurance company recruiter is handicapped on those campuses where prior "missionary" work by the faculty has been ineffective.

3. POPULARITY OF HOME OFFICE EMPLOYMENT COMPARED WITH THAT OF OTHER PHASES OF INSURANCE WORK

Recruiters for life insurance company home office positions compete for new college graduates not only against other branches of business, but also against those offering opportunities in other phases of insurance, namely, life insurance sales positions, and sales and non-sales aspects of property and casualty insurance.

Placement officers agree, almost unanimously, that it is easier to recruit for non-sales than for sales positions in life insurance. Of the 65 officers polled, only 2 stated that life insurance sales positions are easier to fill than non-sales positions, and 3 others find little difference in their relative popularity.

While life insurance home office positions are favored over life insurance sales positions, 33 out of 56 placement directors giving this information believe that property and casualty companies are more popular with their students than are life insurance companies. Eleven maintain that there is no significant difference in their popularity, while only 4 have found life insurance companies to be the more popular.

The principal reason cited by placement people for the superior appeal of property and casualty companies is an old story: most students identify life insurance with sales, and they are "terrified of life insurances sales." A leading property and casualty company has exploited this situation in a recruiting movie which seeks to explain that employment in its own organization involves administrative and technical work rather than selling.

Some placement officers noted that fire and casualty companies frequently have better recruiting techniques and better training programs and offer more interesting employment, than life insurance companies. Placement officers agree, however, that the best recruiting and training programs established by life companies are by no means inferior to the best provided by the fire and casualty firms. And, as is the case in life insurance, no more than a handful of fire and casualty firms have organized extensive recruiting and training programs for college graduates.

At one university the placement director noted that the insurance faculty is more interested in property and casualty than in life insurance because the former offers a wider variety of technical problems. This, he believes, is an important influence steering graduates away from life insurance. No evidence of the extent to which this is typical of insurance faculties throughout the country was gathered in this study.

On the other hand, fire and casualty firms are at a disadvantage in that they are less well known to undergraduates than the leading life companies. While the giant life insurance companies are familiar to everyone, a surprisingly small number of students have heard of their counterparts in the property and casualty industry.

Several of the outstanding property and casualty companies, furthermore, use a recruiting technique which makes them less potent competitors with the life companies than they otherwise would be. These companies use a negative approach, playing "hard to get" with "diabolic" application forms and an unusually arduous selection procedure. The starting salaries offered by these companies are deliberately set below the going rate. By such methods they hope to get only applicants who are so anxious for employment with their companies that they will stay with them for a long time. As a matter of fact, some of these companies have left the market completely during the extremely inflated conditions of the past two years because they feel that a competitive starting salary would have to be too far out of line with their internal salary structure. On the other hand, there are fire and casualty companies which offer starting salaries which equal and often exceed those offered by life companies.

Placement officers and company personnel people agree, however, that life insurance companies are not, as a rule, competing with fire and casualty companies for the services of a well-defined group of college graduates specially trained for and dedicated to a career in insurance. Rather, Armstrong Cork, General Electric, and other such firms in all branches of industry appeal most effectively to the more desirable candidates for home office positions. The validity of this contention is evidenced by the nature of the jobs taken by 65 recent college graduates who refused offers of employment in life insurance company home offices. Of the 38 male graduates responding to a questionnaire, 18 went into manufacturing industries; 4 into banking; 4 into other insurance company home offices; 3 into public utilities; 2 into merchandising; and the remainder went into miscellaneous occupations, including graduate study. The 27 females took an even greater variety of positions: 5 went into industrial firms, 2 joined other insurance firms, 2 went into publishing, 2 into banking, 2 into advertising, 2 into government work, 2 into public service corporations, and the rest went into a miscellany of organizations. Significant here is the preponderance of manufacturing positions taken, particularly by the men. Life insurance companies, to compete successfully for their share of college graduates, evidently should offer opportunities as attractive as those which the leading industrial firms, and not merely other insurance companies, offer.

4. WHY COLLEGE GRADUATES REFUSE HOME OFFICE EMPLOYMENT

The recent college graduates who rejected home office positions were asked to indicate the critical factors causing them to seek employment elsewhere. Most important of these factors are: (1) starting salary, (2) opportunities for advancement in salary, (3) opportunities for advancement in responsibility, (4) nature of the work, and (5) size of the firm. Other factors such as location and growth prospects of the firm or the industry were mentioned by only a few individuals. Because their names were obtained from only five companies, all of which are leaders in college recruitment and training, no respondent singled out the type of selection process or the training as a critical factor.

a. *Starting Salary*

Of 36 male graduates who expressed an opinion, 19 felt that a low starting salary was a major factor causing them to take a position outside of insurance. One man wrote that "a married student can't live on what is offered." Another stated that "insurance companies today hold vast amounts of wealth and yet they are not willing to pay 'going' wages in most cases. They're inclined to be conservative and do not put themselves forth in such a manner as to attract high calibre men." Another student, who made favorable comments about one company's training program and its personnel officer, queried, "If the company thinks the job is worth so little, compared to other industries, why should I value it any higher?" Another indicated that a $75-per-month disadvantage in starting salary made work in insurance "unthinkable."

On the other hand, 15 of the 36 did not consider the starting salary to be a critical factor, even though many of these pointed out that the insurance company offered less than they received in the position they accepted. Thus one student wrote that the starting salary was "unimportant, except it had to be at least $3,000, unless very exceptional opportunity." Another said that it is "fair to about even with what I now receive, but not a deciding factor." And another stated:

"Could have been better, but good or at least on a par with the average salary stated in the spring interviews—should not be a critical factor."

Fifteen of the 27 female college graduates who refused life insurance home office positions were dissatisfied with the starting salary. Said one: "It's too low for dull work." Others complained that it would be insufficient for living away from home. And one quipped: "Working conditions are excellent, hours are very good, but you can't take them home in a pay envelope." Five of the girls did not comment at all on starting salary, while four expressed their satisfaction with the salary, pointing to other factors which made them refuse the positions. One young lady frankly admitted that she was willing to accept the insurance company's salary offer, and was surprised to receive more in another company.

How did the starting salaries of the positions actually taken by this group of graduates compare with those offered by the insurance companies?

Twenty-eight out of 31 males supplying this information took jobs at higher starting salaries than were offered by the insurance companies; 2 accepted the same salary; 1 man took less. In the case of the 23 female graduates responding to this question, 15 were able to obtain more money; 1 took a job for the same salary; and 7 young ladies went to work for less money than they had been offered in insurance. Table 10 shows that the insurance companies whose job offers were turned down by the graduates had starting salaries clustering between $250 and $300 per month for the men and between $200 and $225 per month for the women:

TABLE 10

STARTING SALARIES OFFERED BY SELECTED INSURANCE COMPANIES, 1952, AS REPORTED BY SAMPLE OF NEW COLLEGE GRADUATES

Monthly Salary	Number of Males	Number of Females
Under $200	—	2
$201- 225	—	16
226- 250	6	1
251- 275	12	4
276- 300	13	—
Total	31	23

Source: Questionnaires sent to college graduates (see Appendix III).

Table 11 shows the distribution of the starting salaries actually taken by the graduates sampled. A much wider dispersion is apparent, with a tendency for male salaries to concentrate about the $275 to $300 range and for the girls to accept between $200 and $250 per month.[3]

TABLE 11

STARTING SALARIES ACCEPTED BY SAMPLE OF NEW COLLEGE GRADUATES, 1952

Monthly Salary	Number of Males	Number of Females
Under $200	—	2
$201- 225	2	8
226- 250	2	9
251- 275	5	5
276- 300	11	2
301- 325	5	—
326- 350	6	1
351 and over	2	—
Total	33	27

Source: Questionnaires sent to college graduates (see Appendix III).

b. *Opportunities for Advancement in Salary*

Many college graduates are content to accept a relatively low starting salary if they feel a given position offers unusual opportunities for advancement in salary. What did our sample of college graduates think about these opportunities in the life insurance companies whose offers of employment they rejected?

Of 38 male respondents, 22 commented on this question. Two indicated that they did not know what the opportunities are. Fifteen felt that the opportunities are not good. Said one, "Advancement in salary appeared too rigid. Ability and hard work didn't seem to matter as much as seniority." Another noted that the insurance company was not specific as to the increases promised, while the government agency with which he took employment promised him an increase to $4200 in nine months. One stated: "In insurance the opportunity for rapid salary advancement is slow, and this did influence my thinking." A man who took a job with an oil company said that after one year in that employ-

3. These salaries appear considerably lower than those offered by industrial firms to graduates of a large Eastern business administration school in June, 1953. Monthly salaries between $325 and $350 are typical.

ment he makes as much as he would after five years with an insurance company. On the other hand, 7 male respondents felt that the opportunities for salary advancement seemed good, or, at any rate, that lack of opportunity here was not a critical factor in causing them to turn away from a career in insurance.

Fifteen of the 27 female questionnaire respondents did not comment on salary advancement opportunity. Those who did were evenly divided as to their opinion, with 6 regarding it favorably and 6 unfavorably. This question, it may be presumed, is not so important for female as it is for male college graduates, since only a relatively small proportion of the former look forward to a lifetime career in insurance.

c. *Opportunities for Advancement in Responsibility*

Closely related to the question of opportunities for advancement in salary is that of opportunities for advancement in responsibility.

Of the 38 male college graduates who had rejected life insurance company offers of employment, 16 failed to include these opportunities among the critical factors causing them to take other positions. Eight indicated that the opportunities for advancement in responsibility looked good to them, while 14 reported that they seemed slow or uncertain. Several expressed a fear of "getting lost" in a large organization. Another remarked that these opportunities are "apparently inadequate" and that they were "not clearly outlined by the interviewer."

The reaction of the female graduates was not dissimilar. Eleven made no comment, and 5 considered advancement opportunities to be good. Six felt they would be poor. One thought advancement depended entirely on seniority. Another thought that she would be "one of many; future improvement seemed like one chance in a million."

It was suggested above that few female college graduates look forward to a lifetime career in insurance. One respondent took vehement objection to this attitude on the part of the company which offered her employment:

> The attitude of the executive in charge of the new program for girls in the ——— Department seemed to be that the two things most important in a job to the female college graduate were: 1. Salary. 2. That the job never be dull or boring. In these two aspects the job ranked very high, but in the phase which I considered the most important—chance for advancement—it ranked very low. The company seemed to be offering a pleasant interim occupation, with no real chance for advancement. . . While the X Life Insur-

ance Company may not consider women as valuable prospects for their positions of higher responsibility, I feel they are losing a great opportunity for good executive material. They will never discover their mistake under their present system, though, for they are appealing to the woman looking for pleasant, interim employment, rather than the one who wishes a career in insurance.

d. *Nature of the Work*

To what extent does the nature of the work cause young college graduates to steer away from employment with life insurance company home offices?

More than half of the group of male college graduates who refused home office positions indicated that the nature of the work they would be called upon to perform was an important factor. Eleven failed to comment on this question, while 5 were favorably impressed by the nature of the work as outlined by the recruiter, rejecting the life company's offer on other grounds. Again, it should be emphasized that this sample is hardly typical of the general run of college graduates as a whole, since it consists of people sufficiently interested in an insurance career to make formal application for employment. Nevertheless, 17 were unhappy as to the nature of the work. Said one student:

> This was definitely the deciding factor as for almost every other reason X Life Insurance Company was superior in my judgment.
>
> Whether or not it was true, I simply could not imagine any job connected with selling insurance and collecting the premiums therefor, be it administrative or otherwise, which would be of sufficient interest to me. In my case, therefore, the company would have to have demonstrated to me how the insurance business was interesting. Banking, on the other hand, particularly in its loan contacts with all types of industry, appealed. To become a loaning officer and thus deal with companies of all varieties provided me with a goal of definite interest. Along with that was the definite feeling that should I want to change to a commercial company, the training obtained in the bank's credit department would be far more useful than training in an insurance company. This analysis may be incorrect, but it is the result of my education and the impressions derived therefrom.

Others feel the work is "too routine," "too specialized," "dull." On the other hand, one man wrote: "Insurance is interesting to me and certainly didn't influence me against accepting a job in insurance." Another wrote that "the nature of the work appealed to me." Another believes the work to be "stimulating and self-satisfying."

Of 27 female respondents, 17 objected to the nature of the work offered by life insurance company home offices; only 4 expressed enthusiasm for it, while 6 failed to comment. The women also referred to the routine nature of the work, that it appeared to be less challenging than other occupations. One young lady wrote:

> It would seem to me that part of the reason people (I, for instance) get offered an insurance job and then refuse is because they send representatives to the college in the spring. With a possible employer there you think, "Why not?" The salary looks good, and in an interview, when you really aren't sure of your field, why should you tell them you have doubts? Thus history majors, etc., go in. But when the job offer actually comes in the mail the grim prospect of "life insurance" looms up. When the world is so full of people, ideas, when your training has had a liberal arts slant, why bury yourself in statistics about how soon people may die?

e. *Growth Prospects*

While placement officers report that most enthusiasm is stirred among the student body by recruiters from the so-called "growth" industries, only one of the graduates who rejected a life insurance company offer felt that the growth prospects of the life insurance industry constituted a critical factor in his choice of employment. According to this man, "This was a critical factor, for with the exception of group insurance I feel that insurance has reached a saturation point as compared with the future of the aluminum industry." This point of view may be contrasted with that expressed in an interview with a group of young college graduates now employed by a leading life insurance company. These men were unanimous in their belief in the continued growth of their firm and of the industry. This, they generally agreed, was the most important reason why they considered their future with the company to be bright.

f. *Size of the Firm*

Only eight of the graduates commented on the size of the firm as a factor in their choice of employment. Almost all the respondents had rejected offers made by extremely large insurance companies. Two felt bigness to be an advantage. Said one: "I like a large organization because I feel it offers more opportunity for the man who wants to give that extra effort 'on the margin'." On the other hand, six graduates, three male and three female, felt the large size of the insurance companies to be a disadvantage. One of these stated that "probably advancement and opportunities would arise more often in a smaller company." A vice-president of a large company, it might be added, gathered the impression from some campus visits that students are not so enthusiastic about working for a large organization as they once were.

g. *Other Factors*

Several graduates objected to the location of the companies, particularly those located in the New York City-Newark area. Their objection was generally based on the high cost of living in these areas, in the light of which the starting salaries offered by the companies appeared inadequate. One man made the point that, in choosing between two employment opportunities of equal attractiveness from all other points of view, he would select the one having a parking lot for employee automobiles, if the other did not.

There was little objection to the recruiting technique of life insurance companies, and several respondents made complimentary remarks about the caliber of the recruiters of the companies they turned down. It should be borne in mind that the names of the respondents were provided only by companies that are leaders in the area of college recruitment. Other companies were unable to comply with a request for similar lists because their recruiting is either too sporadic or too decentralized for such lists to be available.

5. WHY COLLEGE GRADUATES ACCEPT HOME OFFICE EMPLOYMENT

Despite the discouraging attitude toward home office employment on the part of college graduates indicated in this chapter, insurance companies are able to secure a substantial number for such positions. The group of college graduates who accepted home office positions were asked how they happened to take this employment.

It is highly significant that, of the 68 employees interviewed, only 7 indicated that they were seriously considering an insurance career as undergraduates, and of these, 5 intended to become actuaries. Three of these stated that a college course in insurance had influenced their decision; only 1 had actually majored in insurance. In addition to the 7, 3 individuals had specialized in finance while in college and were consciously heading toward a career with a financial institution. They found better opportunity in the investment department of a life insurance company than in a bank.

The remaining 58 employees interviewed had not consciously prepared for insurance work while in college. Fourteen of them were recruited on the campus, and took the insurance job in preference to opportunities in a number of other lines of business. Several mentioned that they were "sold" by the personality of the recruiter.[4] One man admitted that he had never even heard of the company, one of the world's largest, before his interview with its recruiter. Eight others were referred to the insurance company by the college placement officer.

Family connections in the insurance business influenced an additional 8 individuals to take home office employment. One man at present occupying an important position in an agency department became an agent for the company because as a chemical engineer he had earned less than a brother-in-law who sold insurance. In many cases, the graduate's father is employed in the home office and has suggested the position.

The remainder of those interviewed "stumbled" upon home office employment for a miscellany of reasons. One man used to walk past the home office building on his way to school. He applied for a job upon graduation because "it seemed like a convenient place to work." Another man had lost his job in California and, recalling that he used to live across the street from an insurance company in Newark, sought a job with the home office where he is now employed. Still another "dropped in" on the home office on the way back from an interview with another company. He had become interested in insurance employment because he discovered these organizations were not so concerned about his draft status as were industrial employers.

Several individuals left banks and casualty companies to work in life insurance. They found the other employment too hidebound, with advancement opportunities usually limited. Others turned to insurance from other employment in a quest for greater job security. For example, an ex-newspaperman took a public relations position in insurance in preference to several higher-paying offers in advertising and magazine publishing.

4. Undoubtedly a greater proportion of the college-level employees interviewed in this study was recruited on the campus than would be true of the industry as a whole because seven of the nine companies revisited have well-organized campus recruiting programs.

❋ *An Appraisal of Home Office Employment Opportunities* ❋

Highlights of Chapter 3

Life insurance company officials believe that the most important advantages of home office employment are: (1) opportunities for advancement, (2) security, (3) good working conditions.

Recent college graduates employed in life insurance home offices also head their list of advantages with "good prospects for advancement." In second place is "nature of the work," followed by "good working conditions," while "job security" ranks fourth.

Low pay as compared with that of industrial employment is considered by officers as well as by recent graduates the principal disadvantage of home office employment.

In 1952, starting salaries offered college graduates by life insurance companies throughout the country averaged between $225 and $250 per month. Larger companies which actively recruited college graduates offered somewhat more.

A "typical" college graduate hired in 1947 enjoyed a salary increase ranging from 75 to 100 per cent during the five-year period ending in 1952. In that year his monthly salary was most frequently reported to be in the $375-$400 bracket. About 80 per cent of male personnel employed five years or more in 50 life insurance company home offices earned more than $5,000 in 1952; 40 per cent exceeded $7,500 in that year.

Large companies tend to pay their male executive, supervisory, and technical employees more than smaller companies do.

Little difference can be found in the salary scales of stock and mutual companies.

✻ *Chapter Three* ✻

AN APPRAISAL OF HOME OFFICE EMPLOYMENT OPPORTUNITIES

THE preceding chapter dealt largely with the attitudes of young college graduates and undergraduates toward home office employment opportunities. Little of this opinion is based on knowledge of the facts of home office employment. This chapter turns, therefore, to the experts on such matters, the company officers and recent graduates employed in the home office, for an objective appraisal of home office employment opportunities.

Life insurance company executives and personnel officials were asked to indicate what they consider the principal advantages and disadvantages of home office employment. Most frequently mentioned—favorably by some and unfavorably by others—are (1) opportunities for advancement; (2) security; (3) working conditions and fringe benefits; (4) salary scale; (5) growth record of the company; and (6) the nature of the work. Included in this discussion is an extensive examination of the salary structure of the life insurance home office. Salary information was obtained from 50 companies and is summarized later in the chapter.

The following table indicates the principal advantages and disadvantages of home office employment mentioned by company officers.

The appraisal of the advantages of home office employment by the group of recent college graduates interviewed is quite similar to that of the officers. Each individual was asked to tell why he had stayed with the company. "Good prospects for advancement," cited 25 times, was the answer most frequently given. The second most frequently offered reason, mentioned 22 times, is the nature of the work. Most of those

TABLE 12

PRINCIPAL ADVANTAGES AND DISADVANTAGES OF LIFE INSURANCE COMPANY HOME OFFICE EMPLOYMENT, CITED BY COMPANY OFFICERS

Advantages	*Number of Times Cited*
Opportunities for advancement	23
Security	17
Good working conditions	15
Excellent growth record	8
Fringe benefits	8
Good salaries	7
Training program	4
Good place to live	4
Small company	2
Broad experience possibilities	1
Opportunity to learn a profession	1
Progressive organization	1
Reputation of company	1
Medium-sized company	1
Mutual company	1
Sympathetic management	1
Ultimate preferment	1
Absence of nepotism	1
Interesting work	1
High *esprit de corps*	1
Prestige	1
Disadvantages	
Relatively low salaries	16
Slow advancement	9
Poor location	2
Large corporation	1
Lack of diversified training program	1
Long training period for key positions	1
Little rotation across department lines	1
Inflexible hours	1
Lack of glamor	1

Source: Questionnaires sent to life insurance company officers (see Appendix I).

interviewed enjoy their particular jobs. Next in order of frequency is "good working conditions." These employees find the home office a good place to work for a variety of reasons: they like the type of people with whom they work; they are respected as individuals; they are treated as equals by the officers, who take a personal interest in their progress. Security ranks fourth. It is particularly important to those with families and of least concern to young, single people.

Ten individuals mentioned salary as a reason why they have stayed in the home office. Most of them regard their salaries as small compared with those paid by industrial firms, but adequate compared with those paid by financial institutions. Several people stated they would not leave the company because they were getting valuable experience, which will be helpful whether or not they make their careers in insurance. Only a handful singled out the fringe benefits, short work-week, and frequent vacations which characterize home office employment, although one or two remarked that this work gives them a greater opportunity to enjoy their families and more time for leisure activities than other, higher-paying occupations. Four individuals declared that an insurance career is gratifying because it fulfills a definite social need.

The college-level employees agreed with the officers on the major disadvantage of home office employment. Most of them think they could be earning considerably more in other lines of business, but remain in home office employment for non-monetary considerations, plus the security and fringe benefits, for which they realize they must give up a substantial number of dollars in salary. Poor location was cited many times, particularly by employees of companies located in New York City. Slow advancement, interestingly enough, was not singled out as a disadvantage of home office employment by any of the graduates interviewed. Over and over again they said: "If I weren't satisfied with my progress up to date, I'd quit." A good number pointed out, however, that other college graduates had become dissatisfied with their progress and had left the company.

When the advantages were weighed against the disadvantages, it was found that an overwhelming majority of those interviewed are glad they chose a life insurance career. Of the 68 sampled, only 4 said they regret their choice and 9 are not sure, principally because they have no experience in other lines of business and cannot make an intelligent comparison.

A further indication of the general contentment of those interviewed is obtained from their replies to the question, "Would you leave your present job for a better opportunity elsewhere at the same or a slightly higher salary?" Only 15 individuals replied in the affirmative; the remainder declared that it would take a much larger salary to move them.

1. OPPORTUNITIES FOR ADVANCEMENT

"Opportunities for advancement" was most frequently mentioned as an advantage of home office employment. At the same time, "slow advancement" is the second most frequently cited disadvantage of home office employment. This illustrates the danger of sweeping generalizations on any of the factors to be discussed in this chapter. Undoubtedly there is a wide variation among companies in terms of advancement opportunities. Furthermore, these opportunities may appear much rosier to those employees who themselves made rapid progress than to others in the same company who have not been pleased with their advancement.

Opinions expressed by officers interviewed were divergent. A personnel official of one very large company asserted that rapidity of promotion in his organization compares favorably with that in any other line of business. He expressed confidence that the college graduate would be able to push ahead in accordance with his demonstrated ability. On the other hand, an executive of another large company indicated that progress up the ladder must be slow. He estimated that of 4,000 home office positions there are only about 150 "good" jobs which are attractive to college graduates. There is high turn-over in the routine, beginners' jobs, but the better positions are usually vacated only by death or retirement. Another mentioned that "a long training period for key positions is necessary," and still another that "advancement in the earlier years may be slow because this is the time the college graduate must be preparing himself with a vast amount of knowledge."

Since company officers agree that the major problem in working with college graduates after they are hired is that of keeping them satisfied until they are ready for promotion, it is surprising to find that a majority of the college-level employees interviewed are generally content with their progress to date and regard their future prospects with considerable optimism. Of the 68 employees interviewed, 39 described their prospects for advancement as "excellent," 7 as "good," and 3 as "fair." On the other hand, 7 believe them to be poor, while 12 are uncertain as to what the future holds for them.[1]

What do these employees believe to be most important factors affecting their future?

Some are confident of their own ability to get ahead, regardless of the conditions prevailing in the company. For example, one young man with two years' experience in underwriting finds there are four people ahead of him in his department, all college graduates. But he feels he should be able to by-pass them in the next few years. Actuarial students, of course, realize that their progress depends almost exclusively on their ability to pass the examinations. Others feel they are fortunate because those employees immediately above them are nearing retirement, while some are discouraged because their immediate superiors are but a few years older than they are. On the other hand, some young people are encouraged because important positions in the company are held by relatively young men, as this indicates to them that they will not have to wait unduly for positions of great responsibility.

In some of the companies visited, the employees were encouraged by opportunities to "go sidewise and up," rather than having to wait until the man ahead of them is promoted or retired. These companies emphasize interdepartmental freedom of movement, while others, particularly the larger and older organizations, do not. In the latter companies, the lack of opportunity to cross divisional or departmental lines disturbs many of those interviewed. A large number of employees, however, have no desire to leave their department, feeling either that their knowledge is too specialized for application elsewhere in the company or that their particular department is growing so fast that opportunities are best for those who remain there.

One individual, with one year's experience in underwriting, feels that his chances for advancement are excellent because the recently

1. At least three sources of bias may have influenced these results. Those employees who have remained with the home office for any length of time can be expected to be relatively satisfied with their progress. In each company the personnel officer selected the employees to be interviewed. While these officers were careful not to "load" the interview schedule with individuals who had made unusual progress with the organization, it is unlikely that they would include a large number of malcontents or misfits. Finally, while those interviewed were encouraged by their personnel people and the writer to speak frankly, on the promise that their individual attitudes would be kept confidential, loyalty to the organization, as well as individual pride of accomplishment, might cause some people to be over-optimistic as to their advancement opportunities.

retired president of the company started in just his position. Those immediately above him are in their early fifties and he is content to wait ten or 15 years for a promotion. Such patience is, however, not typical of those interviewed. Many indicated that they are content because their progress thus far and their prospects for the future are satisfactory, but that if they find themselves in the same position in two or five years, they will look for another opportunity elsewhere.

Two contrasting patterns of advancement evidence themselves. In some companies, employees report that advancement is slow during the first three years. If the individual with real ability is patient during his time, he will enjoy rapid progress thereafter. In other companies, progress, in terms of added responsibility and of increased salary, is quite satisfactory during the first five years, after which a plateau is reached from which it is difficult to foresee further advancement in the very near future. The latter situation seems to obtain where there is little or no opportunity to leave the division in which the employee was trained for openings in other parts of the company.

Most of those interviewed were optimistic about their future because the life insurance home office adheres fairly rigidly to a promotion-from-within policy. The employees sampled agree three-to-one that their top management will not go outside the organization to fill a vacancy unless there is no one within the organization qualified to take it over. This is particularly true of lower-level supervisory and technical positions. In one company, a recent change in top-level management had brought a significant number of new people into the organization at high levels. This was disturbing to many of the employees interviewed, particularly those with several years' service. On the other hand, at least one young man believes that his company overemphasizes promotion from within. He feels new blood should be brought into an organization from time to time lest it stagnate.

Opinions differ as to the effect of company size on advancement opportunities. Some believe that it is too easy to get "lost in the shuffle" in the very large organizations and to become "pigeonholed" in dead-end jobs. They feel there is a greater opportunity to "grow" with the expansion of the smaller company. Others are of the opinion, however, that there are more promotion opportunities in large companies, and, while it takes longer to get a better job in a large company, more good jobs are available. An extremely self-confident individual prefers the larger company because "there is more money at the top." Only a very few employees of the small and medium-sized companies interviewed wished to join larger companies, while a substantial minority of the large-company employees would rather work in a smaller organization.

Are the opportunities for advancement of the young college graduate hampered because seniority plays a dominant part in home office promotion policy?

Insurance company officials differ as to the importance of seniority in their organizations. Some feel it is highly important. Others declared flatly that seniority has no place at all in promotion decisions. Several cases were cited of companies which have undergone widespread reorganization in top management. This has frequently been accompanied by a dramatic shift from promotions based almost entirely on seniority to a complete disregard of this factor.

Included in the questionnaire sent to company officers was the question: "How important is seniority in your company's policy on promotion?" Of 41 companies replying, 11 indicated that it is "important," while 17 reported that it is relatively unimportant. The remaining 13 replied that seniority is considered when all other factors are equal. This last statement is difficult to interpret without an intimate study of actual promotion procedure within each company. To the extent that these answers may be taken at face value, it would appear that seniority is of minor importance in most life insurance company home office promotion decisions and should not interfere with the advancement of young college graduates.

This is supported by the testimony of the young college-level employees. Of 52 individuals who ventured an opinion, 40 believe that seniority is not of major importance in promotion decisions in their company, while 12 believe that it is. Many pointed out that seniority is relatively unimportant in those departments which employ large numbers of college-level people, such as group, actuarial, investments, and methods, but that it is relatively important in departments where large numbers of non-college people perform mass operations. Because of its newness in many companies, the group department seems to be staffed with a particularly young supervisory and officer corps.

2. SECURITY

There is probably no commercial employment which offers greater stability and security than a life insurance company home office position.[2] There are, of course, no seasonal layoffs in this industry, and home office employment is as secure against termination in times of depression as any other. As a matter of fact, some companies reported that they actually added to their home office staff during the last depression, to take care of the increased volume of policy loans. Most insurance companies, however, did experience a decline in employment; but this was accomplished by not filling vacancies as they occurred, rather than by dismissing employees. Company officers recall that few new employees were hired, and promotions and pay increases were few and far between, but wholesale dismissals were unknown.

Practically all the college-level employees interviewed feel that they have great job security. Many of them contend that their company literally never fires anyone. Others are of the opinion that they would have to "shoot a vice-president" to be separated from their jobs. Those who were not absolutely confident that they had a job in the home office as long as they wanted it included one or two with only a few months' service, and several individuals with several years' service who had reached positions of great responsibility. The latter believe that if they fail to show good results in their present capacity, they will be relegated to a dead-end, routine position which will force them to leave the company.

The employees were then asked if job security is important to them. Of the 68 interviewed, 29 replied that it is very important; 20 said that it is of some importance; and 19 avowed that it is of little importance. Most of the young people interviewed were somewhat reluctant to admit that security matters greatly to them. They feel that they should have enough self-confidence to be certain of getting another job should they be dismissed from their present position. Many of them were undoubtedly reacting to the often-repeated charge that today's college graduate is too security-conscious. Although 15 of the 68 mentioned security as one of the reasons why they have stayed in home office employment, only 8 listed it as the most important reason. These, for the most part, are older people with heavy family responsibilities.

2. Small stock companies may be an exception to this statement. Occasionally, drastic changes in personnel, particularly in higher echelons, follow a transfer of controlling interest in the stock.

3. WORKING CONDITIONS AND FRINGE BENEFITS

Working conditions are generally considered ideal in most insurance company home offices. The work-week is often shorter than in comparable white collar jobs, typically running from 35 to 37½ hours. An executive of one Southern company reports that, contrary to the experience of other life companies, he has a waiting list of applicants for clerical positions because of his organization's 36½-hour week. Furthermore, most home offices observe an unusual number of legal holidays.

The most frequent complaints about physical conditions are overcrowding—in the case of companies which have outgrown their home office building—and lack of air conditioning. Many small and medium-sized companies have remedied these defects by leaving their original urban location for modern, suburban home offices. Where this involves a transportation problem for the clerical staff, bus service is often provided.

The employees interviewed gave as the main reason for their satisfaction, not the short hours nor the attractive physical layout of the building, but the pleasant working relationships with their fellow employees and their supervisors. One person reported that department heads take a genuine interest in those under their direction as individuals, and are not merely concerned with getting the work out. Company atmosphere, in the experience of most of those interviewed, tends to be friendly, informal, and relaxed.

Occasional criticism is heard of working conditions in the extremely large companies. There tends to be an oppressive amount of regimentation which, according to one former employee, made him feel that he was still in the Army. He objected to the fact that members of each section went to lunch with the ringing of a bell and had to be back at their desks at the sound of another bell exactly 36½ minutes later. He objected also to the plain-clothes guards who stopped employees leaving the building during working hours until they could produce a pass. He admits that a certain amount of regimentation is necessary to control many thousands of employees at work in the same buildings, but considers it an important reason why he left the employ of the large company. On the other hand, only a few college-level employees who have remained with large companies object to the regimentation. Several indicated that they did at first, but on assuming supervisory responsibility, they recognized the need for the regulations in force.

As was noted above in connection with advancement opportunities, many of the smaller-company employees fear a loss of individuality if they were to join a large organization. Most of the large-company employees interviewed believe this fear to be unfounded, at least as far as their own situation is concerned. They find that the departmentalization which characterizes the large company gives each employee a sense of belonging to a small group in which he is recognized as an individual.

Liberal fringe benefits characterize many life insurance company employee programs. These include group life, sickness, and accident insurance (often provided free of charge by the employer), liberal sick leave, and pension plans. One company even pays for part of the employees' automobile insurance, a practice which was started for the agents and extended to cover home office employees. Many companies, particularly in the metropolitan New York City area, provide free lunches for employees, and others subsidize the operations of low-cost cafeterias. Actuaries of two companies estimate that each provides fringe benefits worth $1,500 annually to each employee. Such benefits must be considered in comparing home office salary scales with those prevailing in other industries. Industrial firms, however, have added so much in fringe benefits in recent years that the life insurance home office is losing its advantage on this score.

4. SALARY STRUCTURE

a. *Starting Salaries*

Home office salaries have been considered previously. It was shown in the preceding chapter that college and university placement officers find starting salaries offered to new college graduates to be less than those of other business areas except financial institutions', advertising agencies', and retailers'. Also, the starting salaries reported by the sample of new college graduates who rejected offers of employment by life insurance home offices clustered between $250 and $300 per month for the men, and between $200 and $225 for the women. Through questionnaires to life insurance company officers, more extensive data on home office salary structure have been gathered.

The starting salaries reported by the sample of graduates are not representative of all companies throughout the country, since they pertain to but a few large organizations in the Northeast which are leaders in college recruitment. A larger sample was obtained from questionnaire responses by company officers. It includes companies of all sizes and in all parts of the country, and reveals a somewhat lower average starting salary, between $226 and $250, with the smaller companies tending to offer slightly less than the larger firms. Table 13 provides this information broken down according to company size. A large proportion of the smaller companies responding to the questionnaire failed to provide this salary information, probably because they rarely hire inexperienced college graduates.

TABLE 13

STARTING SALARIES FOR LIFE INSURANCE COMPANY HOME OFFICE POSITIONS PAID TO INEXPERIENCED COLLEGE GRADUATES WITHOUT SPECIAL TRAINING, 1952

Number of Companies

Monthly Salary	*All Companies*	*Assets (in millions of dollars)* Under 50	50-100	100-250	250-500	500-1,000	Over 1,000
Under $200	—	—	—	—	—	—	—
200- 225	7	1	1	3	2	—	—
226- 250	21	1	8	5	3	1	3
251- 275	9	3	—	1	1	2	2
276- 300	4	—	—	—	1	—	3
Totals	41	5	9	9	7	3	8

Source: Questionnaires sent to life insurance company officers (see Appendix I).

Classification of the data by location of home office failed to reveal significant difference in starting salaries offered by companies in different parts of the nation. A perceptible tendency for those in the Northeast to pay more is probably due to the fact that most of the billion-dollar companies sampled are in this region. The number of companies sampled is too small to draw valid conclusions on geographical differences.

Companies hiring actuarial trainees offer them a somewhat larger starting salary than they give to college graduates without special training. As can be seen from Table 14, $276 to $300 is the most frequently cited salary range for actuarial trainees who have not passed any Society of Actuaries examinations. Only one company reported more than this, however, while more than half the companies indicated that they were offering less.

The companies were also asked what they paid actuarial trainees with three examinations passed. Those universities offering majors in actuarial science, and occasionally others, have graduates who have completed the first three actuarial examinations. Seven companies reported that they start such trainees in the $301-$325 bracket; and six, in the $326-$350 range. Two companies offered less than $300 per month and one was willing to pay more than $350. As there are relatively few college graduates who have successfully completed three examinations prior to entering an insurance company home office, most of the companies failed to state salaries for such individuals.

TABLE 14

STARTING SALARIES PAID BY SELECTED LIFE INSURANCE COMPANIES TO ACTUARIAL TRAINEES WITH NO ACTUARIAL EXAMINATIONS PASSED, 1952

Monthly Salary	Number of Companies
$200-225	2
226-250	6
251-275	5
276-300	10
301-325	1
Total	24

Source: Questionnaires sent to life insurance company officers (see Appendix I).

Some companies have had experience in hiring holders of master's degrees in business administration. Only 11 companies reported starting salary figures for them. These figures are not significantly different from the salaries paid to actuarial trainees with no examinations passed, but are somewhat higher than those paid to holders of bachelor's degrees who have no special training. It is the practice of at least one leading company to pay no more for a graduate degree unless the position specifically requires it. The distribution of salaries paid to masters of business administration is given in Table 15.

TABLE 15

STARTING SALARIES PAID BY SELECTED LIFE INSURANCE COMPANIES TO HOLDERS OF THE DEGREE OF MASTER OF BUSINESS ADMINISTRATION, 1952

Monthly Salary	Number of Companies
$200-225	—
226-250	2
251-275	3
276-300	4
301-325	2
326-350	—
351-400	1
Total	12

Source: Questionnaires sent to life insurance company officers (see Appendix I).

b. *Opportunities for Advancement in Salary*

A majority of the graduates who rejected life insurance positions felt that opportunities for salary advancement in a home office are not so good as those in other fields of business. This opinion is echoed by company officers themselves, since "low salaries" is the most frequently mentioned disadvantage of home office employment, followed by "slow advancement" in second place. A number of officers noted that opportunities for spectacular advances in salary are much better in life insurance selling than in home office non-sales work.

Those college-level home office employees interviewed are not, on the whole, profoundly displeased either with their present salary or with their prospects for salary advancement. Of the 68 interviewed, 29 indicated that they are definitely pleased with their rate of compensation, and 31 are neither particularly pleased nor particularly displeased with their salary. The remaining 8 are definitely unhappy over the amount they are paid. Several remarked that while the high cost of living makes it difficult to make ends meet on their salary, nonetheless they feel they are being paid what they are worth. One young man is content to supplement his salary with part-time employment after working hours, believing he will eventually be rewarded by substantial salary increases if he is patient.

A somewhat larger proportion of those interviewed are definitely pleased with their prospects for advancement in salary. Thirty-five are quite pleased by these prospects, 16 are neither pleased nor displeased, 9 are unhappy, while another 8 cannot tell what those prospects are. In most of the companies in which employees were interviewed, a series of annual salary reviews is in effect. Although these increases are fairly substantial, the employees look to promotional increases to satisfy their ambitions in terms of salary. Some people suggested that smaller semi-annual increases be substituted for larger annual increases. This would tend, they feel, to keep some of the younger employees from getting discouraged between anniversary dates.

Many of the young people interviewed declared that they "don't expect to get rich" in the life insurance company home office. They hope for enough to have a house and a car and to raise a family in comfortable circumstances. One man with two years' service has set his sights on an ultimate salary of $7,200 per year. He said he is not aiming for the $10,000-$15,000 bracket. On the other hand, a man with one year's experience in the same company hopes to be making $8,000 in four or five years.

In some companies, very rapid salary advancement is made during the first few years of employment, after which the prospects for further increases are less encouraging. For example, it is typical of college trainees in one large company to advance from $65 per week to $98 per week in a year and a half. One employee of this company doubled his salary in his first two years. In other companies, the employees must be patient with relatively low salaries during the first three years in the expectation of substantial increases thereafter.

In order that opportunities for salary advancement might be measured, company officers were asked to indicate the approximate 1952 salary of a male college graduate, hired in 1947, who had made average progress with the company. They were also asked to report the salary at which he started in 1947 so that a five-year percentage increase could be calculated.

Forty-two companies provided information on the 1952 salary of an average male college graduate hired in 1947. None reported paying less than $300 per month and seven companies reported a monthly salary in excess of $450. Salaries in the $376 to $400 bracket were most frequently mentioned. The distribution of the salaries is shown in Table 16:

TABLE 16

1952 SALARIES OF "AVERAGE" MALE COLLEGE GRADUATE HIRED IN 1947 FOR LIFE INSURANCE COMPANY HOME OFFICE EMPLOYMENT

Monthly Salary	Number of Companies
Under $300	0
300-325	6
326-350	5
351-375	6
376-400	11
401-425	6
426-450	2
Over 450	7
Total	43

Source: Questionnaires sent to life insurance company officers (see Appendix I).

When these figures are classified by size of company, a tendency for higher salaries to be paid by the larger companies can be discerned;

but the pattern is not consistent. For example, while one company with assets of less than $50 million reported that its "average" college-trained employee who had been with the company five years was paid over $450 per month, no company in the $500,000 to $1 billion class reported a monthly salary in excess of $400. The sample of companies also fails to reveal any salary pattern along geographical lines.

It was possible to calculate the percentage increase in salary over a five-year period from data provided by 34 companies. While six reported increases ranging between 26 and 50 per cent, two indicated a five-year increase exceeding 100 per cent. The largest number reported increases between 76 and 100 per cent. Table 17 presents these data:

TABLE 17

PERCENTAGE INCREASE IN SALARY, 1947-1952, FOR "AVERAGE" COLLEGE GRADUATE EMPLOYED IN LIFE INSURANCE COMPANY HOME OFFICE

Per Cent Increase	Number of Companies
0- 25	0
26- 50	6
51- 75	8
76-100	18
Over 100	2
Total	34

Source: Questionnaires sent to life insurance company officers (see Appendix I).

How does the salary earned by the "average" college graduate in a life insurance company home office after five years compare with that paid in other branches of business and industry? Fortunately, a meaningful comparison can be made, since the identical question was asked of 106 companies in diversified industries by Frank S. Endicott, Director of Placement at Northwestern University.[3] According to his figures, which are based on the records of 3,288 college men entering employment in 1947, the average 1952 salary was $430 per month for men in engineering, $414 per month for those in accounting, $443 for those in sales, and $403 per month for those starting in general training programs. The widest range of present five-year salaries was reported in sales. It runs from $265 per month up to $650. The narrowest range is found

3. "Trends in the Employment of College and University Graduates in Business and Industry, 1952," *Journal of College Placement,* XII (May 1952), 42-47.

among those who entered a general training program: from $300 to $500 per month.

With 1952 salaries for five-year college graduate employees of life insurance companies averaging somewhere between $375 and $400 per month, it is apparent that their classmates who went into other branches of industry, especially into sales and engineering, were doing somewhat better dollarwise. On the other hand, the pay received by accountants and by graduates of general administrative training programs is not appreciably higher.

Mr. Endicott also determined the percentage increase in salary between 1947 and 1952 for "average" college graduates in all lines of industry. The average percentage increase in engineering was 76, compared with 79 per cent for accountants, 97 per cent for salesmen, and 81 per cent for those who started in general training programs. As one can see from Table 16, more than half the life insurance companies supplying this information reported a five-year percentage increase ranging between 75 and 100 per cent. As a matter of fact, a large majority of those companies report increases of between 90 and 100 per cent. On the basis of these figures, one might question the apparently widespread notion that salary advancement in the home offices of life insurance companies is considerably slower than in other fields.

As several personnel people have pointed out, it is difficult for an individual to make a meteoric advancement in salary in a home office, while this is possible in a field such as advertising. It is the performance of a few conspicuously successful individuals in other fields, rather than of the average employee, which gains attention, and which leads to the notion that opportunities for salary advancement are much better outside the life insurance company home office.

College graduates hired today should not necessarily expect to duplicate the 90 to 100 per cent five-year salary advance reported for those hired in 1947. First of all, starting salaries today are materially higher than they were in 1947, so that a comparable percentage increase in the next five years will be much more difficult. It may well be, also, that the relatively good showing in terms of percentage increase made by the home office employee came about because he started in 1947 at a lower salary than those in other branches of business. Secondly, the period from 1947 to 1952 saw a substantial increase in the price level, with concomitant cost-of-living salary adjustments. One cannot safely assume a continuation of the inflationary spiral for the next five years.

c. *Salaries for Males with Five Years of Service or More*

It is widely believed by those in the industry and outside it that the salary structure of life insurance companies is materially below that of other lines of business. In order that objective data on this question might be gathered, the life insurance companies were asked to indicate the number of male employees, having five or more years of service, in each of eight salary categories, starting with "under $5,000" and rising to "$25,000 and over." Fifty companies supplied these data, and the percentage of employees in each salary bracket was computed. By eliminating those with less than five years' service from this survey, trainees and casual employees are excluded. Female employees are likewise excluded, since most of them serve in purely clerical capacities. The resulting sample is intended to consist of career people in technical, supervisory, and executive positions which the male college graduate accepting home office employment hopes eventually to occupy. Table 18 summarizes these data for the entire sample and includes a similar break-down for group sales personnel and for salaried agency management staff.

TABLE 18

Salary Distribution for Male Employees with Five or More Years' Service, 50 Life Insurance Companies, 1952 *

	Home Office	*Field*	
	Executive, Supervisory, or Technical †	Group Sales & Service	Agency Management Staff
Annual Salary	*Per Cent of Employees Earning:*		
Less than $ 5,000	20.2	24.9	10.4
Less than 6,000	40.3	48.0	25.3
Less than 7,500	59.9	80.5	49.2
Less than 10,000	77.9	95.4	75.5
Less than 15,000	90.2	99.9	90.3
Less than 20,000	95.0	100.0	95.1
Less than 25,000	97.2		97.3

* *Characteristics of Sample:*
31 stock companies; 19 mutual companies
17 in Northeast; 3 in Northwest; 7 in Southeast; 8 in Southwest; 15 in Midwest
Asset sizes of companies: 10, under $50 million; 7, $50-100 million; 11, $100-250 million; 10, $250-500 million; 5, $500-1,000 million; 7, over $1 billion

† Excluding printing, building maintenance, and lunchroom staffs.

Source: Questionnaires sent to life insurance company officers (see Appendix I).

This sample is not claimed to be representative of all life insurance companies in the nation. It is weighted heavily in favor of the larger companies. (This objection is mitigated somewhat by the failure to include data of the three largest companies, and of the fifth and ninth in asset size.) Furthermore, the geographic distribution of companies in the sample does not correspond very closely with the actual distribution of companies in the nation.

Despite the shortcomings of the sample, some observations can be made from Table 18. From these figures it appears that some 80 per cent of all males employed five years or more in the home office of a life insurance company were paid over $5,000 yearly, and 40 per cent were paid $7,500 or more in 1952. In terms of the labor force as a whole, these data do not indicate that insurance company home office employees are underpaid. It is noteworthy that those engaged in group sales and service show lower salaries all along the line than the general run of home office employees. Several of the questionnaire respondents indicated, however, that bonus and commission arrangements augment the salaries they reported. Furthermore, the group sales and service personnel may be younger than the average for all home office employees and thus earn somewhat less, since many of the companies have only recently entered the group field. The agency management staff, on the other hand, tends to be better paid than the home office staff, particularly at the lower levels. Only 25 per cent of those in agency management made under $7,500, compared with 40 per cent in the home office. At the higher levels, the salary scales of the two groups are similar. About 10 per cent of both the home office staff and the agency management staff drew salaries in excess of $15,000.

Do larger companies tend to pay higher salaries than small ones? Salary data for the home office and agency management staffs of seven companies having assets in excess of $1 billion and of 17 organizations with assets under $100 million are compared in Table 19.

From these data one can see that, while more than 40 per cent of male home office employees having five or more years of service received less than $5,000 from the smaller companies, only about 16 per cent of the billon-dollar company employees made less than this amount. On the other hand, this sample indicates that about 20 per cent of the employees of both the large and the small companies made in excess of $10,000.

Obviously the billion-dollar companies have a greater number of employees who are paid substantial salaries than the small ones. In the sample on which Table 19 is based, the 7 billion-dollar companies together reported 508 positions paying in excess of $10,000, while the 17 small companies together reported only 85 similar jobs. There are many junior officers and division managers of giant companies who are paid more than the vice-presidents, and even presidents, of small companies. No doubt the $150,000 salary of the president of a leading company equals the entire payroll of a tiny organization. But the fact remains, if these data are not misleading, that once the $10,000 per year mark is crossed, the small companies made as good a showing as the large on a percentage basis.

TABLE 19

SALARY DISTRIBUTION FOR MALE EMPLOYEES WITH FIVE OR MORE YEARS' SERVICE, 7 LIFE INSURANCE COMPANIES WITH ASSETS EXCEEDING $1 BILLION AND 17 COMPANIES WITH ASSETS UNDER $100 MILLION, 1952 *

	Home Office		*Field*	
	Executive, Supervisory, or Technical		Agency Management Staff	
	Over $1 Billion	*Under $100 Million*	*Over $1 Billion*	*Under $100 Million*
Annual Salary	Per Cent of Employees Earning:			
Less than $ 5,000	16.1	40.4	2.6	11.2
Less than 6,000	39.3	53.0	12.3	38.7
Less than 7,500	61.3	66.5	36.8	66.2
Less than 10,000	79.8	79.8	69.0	87.6
Less than 15,000	91.8	90.7	88.5	97.8
Less than 20,000	95.8	94.5	93.8	100.0
Less than 25,000	97.6	96.2	96.6	

* 7 companies with assets exceeding $1 billion include 6 mutuals and 1 stock company; 17 companies with assets less than $100 million include 3 mutuals and 14 stock companies.
Source: Questionnaires sent to life insurance company officers (see Appendix I).

Among the agency management staff, it appears that at all levels employees of the billion-dollar companies receive higher compensation than those of the smaller companies. Because so few of the small companies reporting maintain separate group sales and service staffs, salary comparisons for these employees could not be made.

Several officials interviewed expressed the opinion that stock companies tend to pay their home office staffs more than mutuals. The data gathered in this survey seem to indicate little difference in pay scales, with the mutuals slightly better. Because most of the mutual companies providing salary information are large and most of the stock companies are small, it was felt that combining that data for these groups as a whole would be misleading, since the influence of size would undoubtedly overshadow the form of legal organization in making salary comparisons. To meet this objection, Table 20 was constructed on the basis of 26 companies, 13 stock and 13 mutual, so selected that the same number of companies of each asset size class is contained in each group:

TABLE 20

SALARY DISTRIBUTION FOR MALE EMPLOYEES WITH FIVE OR MORE YEARS' SERVICE, 13 MUTUAL LIFE INSURANCE COMPANIES AND 13 STOCK LIFE INSURANCE COMPANIES, 1952 *

	Home Office		*Field*	
	Executive, Supervisory or Technical		Agency Management Staff	
	Mutual	*Stock*	*Mutual*	*Stock*
Annual Salary	Per Cent of Employees Earning:			
Less than $ 5,000	15.7	18.5	42.4	10.2
Less than $ 6,000	32.8	38.8	53.9	24.8
Less than $ 7,500	53.0	58.0	61.6	52.3
Less than $10,000	71.8	77.5	77.0	82.7
Less than $15,000	85.9	90.2	92.4	95.7
Less than $20,000	92.7	95.4	96.2	98.4
Less than $25,000	96.0	97.5	96.2	99.1

* Each sample contains 3 companies with assets less than $50 million; 2 with assets of $100-250 million; 5, $250-500 million; 2, $500-1,000 million; 1, over $1 billion.
Source: Questionnaires sent to life insurance company officers (see Appendix I).

As can be seen from Table 20, slightly more than 18 per cent of the males employed five years or more by stock companies were paid less than $5,000 per year, while slightly under 16 per cent of mutual employees received less than this amount. The pattern is consistent in all salary brackets for home office employees; a somewhat higher percentage of stock company employees than mutual employees received less than a given salary. But the differences are so slight that one should hesitate to conclude on this evidence that mutuals pay better wages than stock companies.

More than 40 per cent of the men on the agency management staff of mutual companies make less than $5,000, compared with only 10.2

per cent of those in stock companies. In fact, more than 50 per cent of the mutual staffs make under $6,000, as against only about 25 per cent of the stock company staffs. But in the brackets above $7,500, the pattern abruptly changes. Twenty-three per cent of mutual agency staff employees earn more than $10,000, while only 17.3 per cent of stock company agency staff employees exceed this figure.

No conclusions are presented on the question of interregional differences in salary scales. In order to make valid comparisons it would be necessary to compare companies of the same size and same form of organization in the five regions by which the data were classified. Unfortunately, the number of companies reporting their salary structure is too small to allow an adequate sample to be prepared on this basis.

d. *Top Executive Compensation*

Finally, how do the salaries paid to life insurance company top executives compare with those paid to their counterparts in other industries?

According to a National Industrial Conference Board Study of executive compensation [4] for 1940 and for 1949, the top three executives of 21 life insurance companies included in the sample were paid less in both years than the top three officers of firms representing 20 other industries. Only the top executives of airlines received less on the average than the highest paid men in the insurance business. The average salary figures for life insurance company top executives are as follows:

	1940	*1949*
No. 1 Man	$32,000	$43,000
No. 2 Man	22,000	29,000
No. 3 Man	17,000	21,000

In contrast, the top executives of four cigarette companies averaged $171,000 in 1940 and $227,000 in 1949. And the third ranking executives of these companies averaged $97,000 in 1940 and $95,000 in 1949.

While life insurance company executive compensation is extremely low in dollar amount and as a percentage of assets held by the companies, it is slightly above average when compared with the companies' annual receipts. In both years the compensation to executives amounted to 0.6 per cent of the life companies' annual income. The median percentage of sales represented by total executive pay for 1949 in the Con-

4. See *Business Week*, Sept. 1, 1951, p. 54.

ference Board study is 0.4. Cigarette company executive compensation, to continue the comparison, amounted to 0.4 per cent of sales in 1940 and to 0.2 per cent of sales in 1949.

5. GROWTH OF THE COMPANY

Several of the officials polled pointed to the excellent growth record of their companies as an important advantage, making opportunties for advancement greater than in organizations where growth is not so spectacular. This is particularly important where large numbers of young college graduates are employed, because growth companies are better able to cope with the new employees' eagerness to advance to new positions of responsibility. As might be expected, employees of smaller companies feel their future is more intimately tied up with the company's growth than do employees of very large organizations.

Observation of a large number of organizations reveals that a life insurance company's recent entry into new lines of coverage opens more job opportunities for college people than mere increases in the amount of ordinary insurance in force. Many companies have recently entered the group and the accident and health fields. This has necessitated the staffing of a wide variety of technical positions. One company reports that half its college-trained employees are engaged in some phase of group insurance. Where reserves of college-level trainees are not available, the company has had to go outside its organization and "pirate" experienced personnel from other companies. A growth in ordinary sales, on the other hand, is generally reflected by a multiplication of routine operations and calls for a minimum of new positions of responsibility. For example, the home office staff of one large company which, up to 1952, wrote ordinary life insurance only, has remained constant in size since 1940, while its insurance in force doubled.

6. NATURE OF THE WORK

A senior executive of a leading company pointed out that the typical large life insurance company has a relatively small percentage of jobs which would be challenging and attractive to intelligent college graduates. In his actuarial department, for instance, there are 20 mathematicians to 500 or 600 employees performing routine operations. The controller's department, employing 700 people, provides less than 20 technical jobs. And while the operation involved in billing and collecting several million premiums annually is one that takes a considerable staff, only one or two people who understand the principles are needed to supervise the entire operation. On the other hand, the investment department consists almost entirely of technicians with a small clerical staff, as does the law department.

College graduates are recruited by this company and by most others for specialized positions, particularly financial, actuarial, underwriting, and accounting. In other areas the mass nature of the work makes it unattractive to college students and, furthermore, the company does not need people of this caliber to perform these jobs.

As was mentioned in the introduction, the great majority of the college-level employees interviewed hold technical rather than supervisory or merely clerical positions. Table 21 represents a summary of the positions held:

TABLE 21

OCCUPATIONS OF COLLEGE-LEVEL HOME OFFICE EMPLOYEES INTERVIEWED *

Position	Number of Employees
Underwriting	11
Methods	10
Actuarial training	9
Security analysis	5
Accounting	4
Agency direction, research	4
Public relations, editing	3
Personnel	3
Cost analysis	3
Auditing	3
Supervisory, clerical operations	3
Mortgage analysis	2
Sales promotion	1
Policy planning	1
Clerical	1
Legal	1
Office services	1
Claims	1
Secretarial	1
Correspondence approver	1

* This table is not intended to reflect the general pattern of positions held by college-level employees of life insurance company home offices. The employees were selected for interviews with the sole purpose of representing as wide a variety of positions and lengths of service as possible.

Source: Interviews with college-level home office employees (see Appendix IV).

Almost without exception, those interviewed enjoy their jobs. This is most significant in view of the typical appraisal of home office work by outsiders as "dull" and "routine." Of the 68 canvassed, 28 declared that the work is a challenge to their full ability almost all the time; 33 find it a challenge some of the time, while only 7 feel that their jobs never present a challenge. Most of the employees admit that they must perform a considerable amount of routine detail work which does become dull. But few find this routine work oppressive, because it is relieved by a variety of more interesting assignments.

As a rule, home office work is not performed under great pressure of deadlines or insistent demands by superiors for ever increasing quality or quantity of work. From the testimony of those interviewed, it is carried out in a comparatively relaxed atmosphere. Fifteen of the 68 individuals interviewed, however, feel that they work under pressure all the time and another 8 said that they are usually under pressure. Thirty-six, on the other hand, are under pressure only occasionally, while 9 feel that they are never under pressure. Quite a few, particularly those in more responsible positions, indicated that any pressure under which they work is self-imposed.

Exactly half of the group stated that their jobs keep them busy all the time, while the other half reported peaks and valleys in the work flow. A frequently repeated complaint is that there is too little to do at times. A young employee of a large company said that he is contented when he is busy, but when he sits around with nothing to do, he begins to feel "like a mere number" in the organization. Other individuals, engaged in staff work, are annoyed at the great amount of time they must spend "waiting around" until the officers and supervisors with whom they work have time to see them.

The employees interviewed were asked to describe the nature of their jobs and their attitudes toward them. It may be worthwhile to paraphrase some of their replies in an effort to give the flavor of home office employment as recent college graduates experience it:

Group Underwriting (Four Years' Service)

This man is a member of the specialized unit handling "trusteed" cases, i.e. insurance policies established by a trustee appointed by the employer and the union as the result of a collective bargaining agreement. He handles policies, checks certificates, and reviews information booklets for employees. He must examine contracts to determine whether they comply with state laws, whether the proper rates are assigned, and whether they conform to proper underwriting practices. Major decisions are referred to his superior, an assistant secretary. He reports that while there is much of a routine nature in group underwriting, there is so much to learn that the work is challenging.

Group Underwriting (Three Years' Service)

The principal task of this employee is to review cases sold in the field. He performs the initial work on difficult cases and checks other underwriters on simple cases. He makes no important policy decisions. A challenging aspect of the work involves his contacts with agents in the field. He must "sell" them on plans which meet home office approval. He experiences a considerable amount of pressure as a result of demands by agents for immediate information and quick decisions in order to meet competition.

Ordinary Underwriting (Two Years' Service)

This man is one of five college graduates being trained as lay underwriting experts, each of whom will be assigned to a different geographical area. After the training period, they will visit agents to interpret new regulations and to act as liaison between the home office and the field. In addition, this employee teaches speed reading and correspondence to clerks in the underwriting department. He reports that underwriting production work sometimes involves dull routine, but he expects it during the first few years. Annual sales campaigns increase the volume of work, which involves overtime.

Methods (One Year's Service)

This relatively recent employee is assigned to the Forms Control Unit. His job is to consult with operating departments in the development of new forms. He engages in some study of systems in order to suggest methods of simplification. There is an irreducible minimum of routine he must face. Since new forms must be ready by specified dates, he is under a moderate amount of pressure most of the time.

Methods (Three Years' Service)

This man engages in home office departmental surveys and audits. These involve work measurement, time studies, organization and supervision studies, and forms design. In his opinion, a good part of the work is challenging, but there is always a considerable amount of "machine punching." He experiences some frustration because lower level supervisors are not prone to change their methods and hence are not receptive to suggestions. He seldom is under pressure and regards the work pace as slow.

Actuarial Training (Three Years' Service)

This man is engaged in a rotation program in the actuarial department. He has spent from nine months to a year in group insurance and group annuities, and in the statistical department. He is not required to master routine jobs and is sometimes given special assignments suitable to his level of training. He complains that no effort is made to acquaint students with other parts of the company so that they could learn how actuaries fit into the overall picture.

Actuarial Training (Two Years' Service)

He is involved in a rotation program which takes him through the dividend section, the mathematical valuation section, mathematical correspondence, and the IBM machine room. The work is arranged to be helpful for examination preparation, but it never challenges his full capacity. He indicates that he is busy all the time, but not under high pressure.

Security Analysis (Five Years' Service)

This specialist analyzes loans to heavy industry. He may visit borrowers in order to interview management. He writes an "offering sheet" which presents loan proposals to an investment committee consisting of officers of the investment department. He supports his proposals by personal appearances before the committee. There is a great diversity of situations to be analyzed which taxes his capacity to the fullest extent.

Accounting (One Year's Service)

He calls himself a "head bookkeeper." He prepares trial balances, checks ledgers, and supervises junior bookkeepers. He estimates that it takes a year before the job becomes routine. He is under some time pressure because of the need to meet statement dates.

Auditing (Eight Months' Service)

This new employee makes internal audits of home office departments and of agencies and mortgage correspondents throughout the country.

The job involves detailed checking of records as well as some study of systems and methods. He studies internal controls to determine whether they are worthwhile or too expensive. Sometimes the work is challenging; sometimes it is routine detail work. He is generally kept busy, but he reports that he is in one of the few departments in the company where he is allowed to read if he has nothing to do.

Public Relations (Seven Years' Service)

This comparatively senior employee is involved in editorial work on house publications and handles press publicity. He has prepared an employee handbook and a leaflet for recruiting part-time clerical help. He feels he is under much pressure in a highly challenging job at which he cannot relax. He loves his work.

Agency Direction (Seven Years' Service)

This man has one of the most responsible positions of those interviewed. He directs a group of agencies, involving organization, selection and training of agents. Much of the work is of a personnel nature. Pressure is generally self-imposed; there are no time deadlines.

Controller's Department (One Year's Service)

Training in the controller's department for this employee is tentatively scheduled for two years and will include four main areas: accounting, premium collection, internal auditing, and policy loans. He learned much in the accounting department, in which he did tax work for the annual statement. He finds the premium collection job less challenging, but he does not mind it. He enjoyed the pressure in the accounting section and indicates that he is bored if not given enough to do every day.

Mortgage Analysis (Three Years' Service)

After only three years' service he is in charge of all mortgages in the Eastern region, except New York City and Boston. He acts as liaison between field and home office. He has responsibility for approval of all loans up to $20,000; above this amount he must obtain approval by a superior. He finds field work a great challenge: he must make snap decisions and deal with people more experienced than he. There is much detail work in the home office.

Policy Planning (Three Months' Service)

This brand-new employee is learning the operation of the policy planning department which handles changes of beneficiary and supplementary contracts. He determines who has rights under policies and recommends endorsements for policy assignment. He answers questions of policyholders and agents on problem cases. He believes the job could become routine, but declares that it is challenging at present while he is still in the learning stage.

Central Filing Department Supervision (Three Years' Service)

This man is manager of the filing department and is in charge of application files, microfilming, and records destruction. This is his first assumption of line authority over a large number of clerical help. He finds personnel problems to be a great challenge.

The employees whose work has been described are technicians and specialists rather than the rank and file of home office employees who perform the many routine clerical tasks necessary in such an organization. Some foresee a radical change in the nature of home office operations which will take place in the next decades. Electronic computers, it is predicted, will displace most of the people performing routine operations. Home offices may eventually be manned by a handful of highly skilled mathematical and electronic technicians in addition to the actuaries, investment analysts, underwriters, and others now performing the technical functions.

7. PRESTIGE

A recent study of the attitudes of college graduates toward employment in retailing reveals that such employment is relatively unattractive because working in a store carries little prestige. Since this seems to demonstrate that prestige may be a significant element in employment-seeking, the group of college-level employees was asked if the prestige of life insurance home office employment is a positive, a neutral, or a negative factor in encouraging young people to seek this career. Exactly half of those interviewed believe the prestige involved to be a neutral factor; the balance are almost evenly divided between answers of "positive" and "negative."

When asked to rate the prestige commanded by life insurance home office employment in comparison with the learned professions and with similar white-collar positions in a large industrial firm, a large bank, and a large department store, most of the group rated insurance employment below the learned professions and industrial employment, on a par with banking, and above retailing.

Some pointed out that the prestige depends primarily upon the position held within the home office: actuaries, and possibly investment and agency department employees, enjoy high prestige, while other positions are regarded by the public as low-paying clerical jobs. In an insurance center such as Hartford, insurance employment rates better in prestige value than it does elsewhere. A number of those interviewed believe that home office employees have greater prestige than insurance agents. Some expressed the opinion that the prestige associated with life insurance work is principally derived from the industry's contribution to the social welfare.

❋ *Recruiting College Graduates* ❋

Highlights of Chapter 4

Most life insurance companies that engage in college recruiting entered such activities after World War II, although seven of the polled companies actively recruited college graduates prior to 1930.

The largest number of companies queried report that they have no formal recruiting plan, but merely receive applications from college graduates who seek them out.

In a substantial number of companies, however, a centralized recruitment office contacts colleges to fill home office positions. Some large companies utilize agency managers to recruit for both home office and field positions, while several leaders in college recruitment procure both field and home office personnel through a home office staff.

College placement officers are favorably impressed, on the whole, with the caliber of the home office recruiter. They are generally pleased, too, with the recruiting literature provided by a few companies, but believe more organizations should distribute this literature.

Some home office employees urge that recruiting begin before the end of the senior year by providing college students with summer employment after their junior year.

* *Chapter Four* *

RECRUITING COLLEGE GRADUATES

THE remainder of this study presents a survey of the principal activities of life insurance companies involving the new college graduate. The present chapter is devoted to recruiting, while the succeeding chapters take up selection, training, placement, and management development of home office personnel.

The number of years life insurance companies have been engaged in formal college recruiting activity is considered in this chapter first. It then deals with a problem which continually arises whenever life insurance company recruiting is discussed with college placement officers, namely, centralized versus decentralized recruiting: should recruiting be carried on by home office personnel exclusively or by branch managers in the field?

Home office recruiting practice is examined to discover the extent to which it is sporadic or continuous, the number of colleges and universities typically visited, and other sources of college graduates. The chapter is next concerned with the relations of the company recruiter and the campus placement officer: a report is given of the recruiter's appraisal of the placement office and the placement officer's appraisal of the life insurance recruiting program. Under this heading are found placement people's opinions on the caliber of the recruiter and on recruiting literature prepared expressly to attract college graduates to home office positions.

1. BEGINNINGS OF COLLEGE RECRUITING

Seven life insurance companies of the 65 polled indicated that they actively recruited college graduates for home office positions prior to

1930, and 11 indicated that they carried on such activities between 1930 and 1941. College recruiting in life insurance, as well as in all other phases of business, came into its own during the post-war period. Seventeen companies reported activity in 1946. During the period from 1950 to 1952, 38 companies engaged in this practice. Thirty-five companies reported that they planned active recruiting in 1953. While these figures show rather extensive college recruiting activity, there is considerable variation among the companies in their actual recruiting operations. At one end of the scale are several companies which maintain a staff whose full-time job it is to make contact with college placement officers; interview hundreds of students; put them through an elaborate screening and induction process; supervise a formal training program; and, finally, arrange for their placement in the line or staff organization of the company. At the other end, there are several companies reporting "active" college recruiting who have no formal plan, but merely receive the employment applications of college graduates who happen to seek them out. Obviously, the elaborate recruiting organization is beyond the means and the needs of a small organization. On the other hand, medium-sized companies are among the leaders in organized college recruiting, and there are very small companies that are also active.

A distinction should be made between recruiting for actuarial trainees and for other home office positions. In most large companies it is a long-standing practice for an actuarial officer to maintain contact with placement officers and mathematics professors in order to hire promising students for actuarial training. The organized recruiting of college graduates for non-actuarial home office positions and, more specifically, for general administrative training programs, is a relatively new departure, although there are at least two companies which have engaged in the latter activity since the 1920's.

2. CENTRALIZED VS. DECENTRALIZED RECRUITING

In industry as a whole there has been a tendency for increasing centralization of college recruiting. Frank S. Endicott [1] reports that of 160 companies queried, 72 indicated that they have moved toward a more centralized plan of recruiting inexperienced college and university graduates, while only 10 moved toward a decentralized plan. Seventy-eight firms have maintained their present plan for many years. The life

1. "Trends in the Employment of College and University Graduates in Business and Industry," *School and College Placement,* IX (Mar. 1949), 57-66.

insurance companies in this study were asked to indicate the extent to which their recruiting activity is centralized. The responses have been tabulated in Table 22.

TABLE 22

LIFE INSURANCE COMPANY PLANS FOR RECRUITING COLLEGE GRADUATES FOR HOME OFFICE POSITIONS, 1952

Description of Plans	Number of Companies *
1. No formal plan. Sufficient number of graduates apply directly to meet company's needs.	26
2. Department heads determine their own needs and sources of new employees. Some may contact colleges, others may not.	2
3. Branch managers recruit for home office as well as for sales positions.	0
4. Recruitment is decentralized, but a central office assists department heads and/or branch managers in contacting colleges.	8
5. Formal recruiting program for actuarial trainees only.	5
6. Centralized recruitment office contacts colleges to fill home office positions.	22
7. Centralized recruitment office contacts colleges to fill both home office and sales positions.	6
8. Other plan.	8

* Four respondents indicated use of more than one plan.

Source: Questionnaire sent to life insurance company officers (see Appendix I) and interviews. Description of plans adapted from Frank S. Endicott, "Trends in the Employment of College and University Graduates in Business and Industry," *School and College Placement,* IX (Mar. 1949), 60.

One company which is highly regarded by college placement people maintains a full-time college recruiting and training staff in the personnel department. In the fall of the year the officer in charge sends out a memorandum to executive officers asking them to have their department heads determine the number of men they will need for the coming year. These requisitions are returned in October, and from November to January the winter graduates are recruited; they are processed in January and February. Spring graduates are recruited in March and April. Campus visits are made by a member of the college recruiting staff accompanied, where possible, by another officer of the company who is a graduate of the institution. In 1952 this company interviewed 1,142 men, of whom 229 were brought to the home office for further interviews and 52 were eventually hired. This organization is one of several in which the home office staff recruits for both sales and non-sales positions.

In 1953 this company embarked on an experiment to increase its campus coverage. The personnel officer in charge of college recruiting gave a series of lectures on recruiting techniques to 30 young home office employees and then sent them back to their own college campuses. These "amateur" recruiters were highly successful in attracting new employees, although the draft situation, coupled with the high starting salaries offered by competing industrial firms, prevented this company from meeting its college-level manpower needs in this year.

Other companies, particularly extremely large ones, sacrifice centralization for breadth of coverage; coordination of recruiting activities is then maintained through efforts of a home office staff. One such company assigns agency managers to the colleges and universities in their immediate locality, with the understanding that only one agency manager of that company may contact a given college. Each manager is instructed to recruit nationally, that is, to screen applicants who wish to settle in other regions and to refer satisfactory candidates to the agency managers in those regions. Graduates interested in home office positions are referred to the appropriate department heads in the home office. A director of college relations in the home office coordinates the recruiting activities of the agency managers. He accompanies the agency managers on their initial visits to placement officers in order to help establish rapport, and instructs them in interviewing techniques.

The fact that so large a number of insurance companies report centralized recruiting is encouraging in the light of the preference of many college placement officers for centralization. Interviews with placement officers of colleges in the South and East brought out extremely strong opinions on this subject. Many placement officials are greatly annoyed when several representatives of the same company, particularly several branch managers or general agents, contact them at various times during the year, each asking that the officer make a special effort to obtain candidates for him. Several placement directors interviewed will not receive more than one representative of a given company.

The opinion was expressed more than once that only a highly placed home office representative can adequately describe to the college student the opportunities available in the home office. Branch managers and general agents, furthermore, incline to stress sales opportunities and play down non-sales positions. On the other hand, the placement directors to whom questionnaires were sent, in 55 colleges and universities throughout the country, apparently are not so one-sided in their preference for centralized home office recruiting as are the Eastern seaboard placement people who were interviewed. Of 54 officials answering this question, 20 indicated that branch managers may successfully recruit for home office positions, while 20 feel they cannot. Another 14 qualified their affirmative answers to this question by such remarks as:

"Perhaps, if they do not try to sell their sales opportunities first."

"Not unless the branch managers are thoroughly integrated with the home office and their decisions final."

"Yes, if they have been indoctrinated sufficiently. But the recruiter who doesn't know the answers is worse than nobody."

"Not unless they have home office experience."

A strong case for centralized recruiting is made by H. Paul Abbott of the Insurance Company of North America. His argument seems as relevant to life insurance as to property and casualty companies:

> Shall we centralize or decentralize the hiring responsibility? I feel this can be largely determined by the form our training takes. If we can afford home office training schools, the responsibility should be centralized so that the calibre of trainees can be measured by a set standard, and this standard should be at least subject to review by the individual or individuals responsible for the formal training process. This does not, however, mean the absence of participation in selection on the part of those responsible for management of local offices, for such would be a grievous error. If we would have branch office managers welcome our product after training, we must be sure they participate actively in recruiting...
>
> If employment authority is decentralized and training likewise, varying standards and results will inevitably follow. Selection and training must then inevitably absorb far more time on the part of the local manager and must constitute a far more important factor in top management's judgment of his worth and effectiveness as a manager. If the manager's primary function is production and supervision of insurance writings in his territory, giving selection and training to a man of lesser stature and insurance knowledge will prove to be false economy. It is a neat trick to teach a fieldman the true worth of selection and training. Moreover, being the producer type, he may tend to "over-sell" job opportunities, interpreting the beginner's opportunities in terms of his own successes and without adequate understanding of the in-

gredients necessary for such success. A good insurance man is not necessarily a good judge of men and not all offices can afford a separate, specialized and trained personnel man. In short, it must be a very small company indeed which cannot afford to consider seriously the centralized method of selection and training control.[2]

In a report prepared for its group policyholders in all phases of business, the Metropolitan Life Insurance Company also advocates centrally-coordinated recruiting:

The recruiters, individuals or in teams, may go out from the company's home office or from local district or division offices. In either case it has proved wisest to have the activity centrally coordinated, usually by the personnel department. Otherwise the company may be embarrassed by having two or more groups recruiting independently on the same campus at the same time.[3]

In more than one company which has recently embarked on a program of college recruiting, there is a mild tug-of-war taking place between the college recruiter in the personnel or the agency department, and heads of the actuarial, underwriting, investment, and other home office departments which require college graduates. The college recruiters, because of the advantages of centralized recruiting, maintain that they can do a satisfactory recruiting job for these departments, the final selection, of course, being left to the department heads. Many of the latter feel, however, that only representatives of their own departments can perform this function, and they refuse to let an outsider do it. In the absence of clear-cut policy laid down by top-management, recruiting remains decentralized in these companies.

3. CONTINUOUS VS. SPORADIC RECRUITING

Placement officers stress the necessity of maintaining a continuing relationship between the company and the placement office so that the officer can get to know the particular type of graduate the recruiter is seeking and can intelligently select people for him to interview. They naturally favor those companies which interview graduates in good years and bad, rather than those which seek college students in boom years only. A "code of ethics" for interviewing procedures that has

2. "Dealing in Futures" (paper presented before Insurance Educational Directors' Conference, Insurance Institute of America, New York, N.Y., June 21, 1949).

3. *Recruiting and Placing College Graduates in Business,* Policyholders Service Bureau, Metropolitan Life Insurance Company (New York, 1950), p. 17.

been widely circulated among recruiters and placement people states that it is an industry responsibility to "visit the colleges regularly, in lean years as well as in good years."[4] Insurance companies, which are less affected by cyclical fluctuations than most other industries, are in a particularly good position to maintain this steady relationship. At least one large insurance company in the property and casualty field follows a "counter-cyclical" recruiting policy. It actively recruits college graduates in recession years and stays out of the market in boom periods, when other industries outbid it in terms of starting salary. This company's recruiting director refers to himself as the placement officer's "foul weather friend."

Of 56 companies from which this information was obtained, 19 reported that they are in continuous contact with one or more college placement offices through actual campus visits; 34 indicated that their contact is sporadic, occurring only as new graduates are needed; 3 reported no contact at all.

The placement officers were asked to report the number of life insurance companies visiting them on an annual or semi-annual basis to recruit graduates for home office positions. The great majority of the officers indicated that not more than 5 or 6 companies maintain a continuing relationship with them, while 2 institutions are visited by more than 20 companies. The replies have been summarized in Table 23:

TABLE 23

NUMBER OF LIFE INSURANCE COMPANIES VISITING COLLEGE AND UNIVERSITY PLACEMENT OFFICES ON AN ANNUAL OR SEMI-ANNUAL BASIS TO RECRUIT FOR HOME OFFICE POSITIONS, 1952

Number of Companies Visiting	Number of Placement Offices Reporting
0- 3	13
4- 7	15
8-11	10
12-15	9
16-20	2
Over 20	2
No information	14
Total	65

Source: Questionnaires sent to college placement officers (see Appendix II).

4. See Stephen Habbe, "College Recruitment in 1952," *Management Record,* XIV (Jan. 1952), 8.

Many life insurance company representatives make campus visits on a sporadic basis. One placement officer estimates that several dozen make occasional visits to the campus. Another facetiously remarked that he is visited by "all of them" at one time or another. Twenty-one of the 65 officers polled reported that more than 20 companies visit them sporadically.

4. NUMBER OF SCHOOLS VISITED

The companies which have not developed a formal program tend to contact only a few local colleges for recruits. Those companies which look for a substantial number of people each year find it necessary to maintain contact with many colleges. In one large company an attempt is made to cover 500 colleges throughout the country. This is done on a decentralized basis by agency managers, coordinated by the home office. Several other companies which have established full-time recruiting staffs visit 40 or 50 colleges a year. As can be seen from Table 24, however, most companies contact but a relatively few colleges each year. This is due, not only to the lack of development of organized recruiting programs, but also to the obvious fact that most of the smaller companies can satisfy their needs for college-trained manpower from a few local colleges.

TABLE 24

NUMBER OF COLLEGES AND UNIVERSITIES CONTACTED IN A TYPICAL YEAR BY LIFE INSURANCE COMPANIES IN RECRUITING FOR HOME OFFICE POSITIONS, 1952

Number of Colleges Contacted in a Typical Year	Number of Companies Reporting
None	4
1- 5	26
6-10	6
11-20	6
More than 20	9
No information	14
Total	65

Source: Questionnaires sent to life insurance company officers (see Appendix I) and interviews.

The placement officer of a large Eastern university is not sure that widespread recruiting by life insurance companies brings the best results. He writes:

It seems to me that life insurance companies should recruit intelligently and aggressively in geographic areas reasonably close to their Home Offices and not scatter their shots too widely. They should endeavor to personalize their relationships with a number of good schools instead of "wholesaling" their needs to a great many. Placement men should know exactly the type of men they want and what they are going to do with them. The placement director can do a great deal for a company if he is thoroughly familiar with a company's needs and is sympathetic to the problems of a good recruiter.

Since most organizations recruit from but a few colleges, it is not surprising that these are located in the immediate vicinity of the company. This is advantageous to both the company and the employee, since the young college graduate who has not established a family of his own need not bear the extra expense of living away from home. Particularly in the South, placement officers remarked on the reluctance of many students to leave their native state. This has hampered the recruiting efforts of companies located elsewhere. The personnel officers polled were asked if they normally recruited from local colleges only, or on a regional or national basis. The results are tabulated in Table 25.

TABLE 25

Location of Colleges Contacted in a Typical Year by Life Insurance Companies in Recruiting for Home Office Positions, 1952

Location of Colleges Contacted	Number of Companies Reporting
Local only	20
Regional	23
National	11
None	4
No information	7
Total	65

Source: Questionnaires sent to life insurance company officers (see Appendix I), and interviews.

5. OTHER SOURCES OF COLLEGE GRADUATES

Campus visits are not the only means which company personnel people have used to recruit college graduates. Seven of the 65 companies report that their contact with the colleges has been maintained by correspondence only; 22 others visit some campuses and merely correspond with others. Several company officers stated that they are generally disappointed with the results obtained by corresponding with placement directors, indicating that personal contact is essential for satisfactory recruiting results.

Of 61 companies providing this information, 13 make use of newspaper advertisements, and 20 of employment agencies, in addition to contacts with placement officers. The remaining 28 use neither source. As is obvious from these figures, opinion is divided on the usefulness of sources other than the campus placement office for new college graduates.

One personnel official expressed the feeling of many others when he stated that the new college graduate who lists himself with an employment agency has been "already pretty much picked over" in interviews arranged by his college placement office. On the other hand, another recruiter finds that certain employment agencies are better equipped than college placement offices to analyze his particular job requirements and make more intelligent selection of candidates for him to interview.

Several company people noted that blind newspaper advertisements are surprisingly good sources today. Of seven men hired for a management training program in the spring of 1952, one company training director obtained four from advertisements in the financial sections of leading newspapers and in specialized financial journals. He reported the greatest volume of responses from advertisements in the newspapers directed at the general reader, but best quality from the financial journals. He found, too, that candidates obtained through advertisements were less likely to refuse a firm offer of employment than were those obtained through college placement officers. Only one candidate out of nine from the latter group accepted his offer, while none of those replying to his advertisement declined an offer. Another recruiter found that the doubling of newspaper advertising expenditures has quadrupled the number of candidates he has been able to hire from this source.

Several company officers noted that they obtain a fairly substantial number of recruits from internal sources. Former trainees provide quite a few candidates from among their college friends. Department managers and agents also recommend individuals.

6. THE RECRUITER APPRAISES THE PLACEMENT OFFICE

How do company personnel officers evaluate their college recruiting experience? By and large they have been favorably impressed with the cooperation extended by the college placement offices. Most of the questionnaire respondents characterized this cooperation as "good," "excellent," and even "splendid." Another commented, however, that he has found "wide variation from poor to excellent, depending upon the school." And another noted that the "tendency of colleges seems to be to favor the large recruiters who recruit every year. This makes it harder for the smaller company that has good opportunities to offer but does not make them in quantity every year."

A top executive of a large insurance company reinstituted a policy of college recruiting for home office positions in 1947. He personally visited the placement officers of several major universities and in some was given an almost hostile reception. This he attributes to the unfavorable impression general agents have made on the college campuses in their recruitment of college-trained insurance salesmen. When this officer was able to make clear that he was recruiting for home office, non-sales positions, his reception improved. Another executive made the same point: college placement officers receive recruiters cordially when they represent the home office, but are less helpful when contact is made from the general agency.

H. Paul Abbott has gone on the record with some penetrating criticism of college placement facilities:

> During the past three years I have been on well over a hundred different college campuses in this country seeking able manpower for a large corporation. It is no exaggeration to state that in fully 90% of these institutions vocational guidance, placement personnel and facilities are woefully inadequate. Of course, the war created situations which were entirely beyond the capacities of educational institutions to meet. To that extent, obviously, the educator must be forgiven. But the problem was present at least to a lesser degree before the war, and as the campus situation returns to normal it can no longer be tolerated....[5]

Just as many college placement officers criticize life insurance recruiting for its lack of centralization, Mr. Abbott points out that many universities are guilty of the same practice:

> Not much better is that to be found in the university where each individual college has its own separate and distinct placement unit completely decentral-

5. "Our Product and Our Problem" (paper presented before conference of placement directors and representatives of industry, Georgia School of Technology, Atlanta, Georgia, Jan. 28, 1949).

ized. There is frequently found no integration of the placement efforts; the left hand knoweth not what the right hand doeth. Indeed, factional jealousies make permanent the situation. Duplication of efforts and limited numbers of personnel widely separated produce highly ineffectual results. To make it worse, the students know the situation and laugh at the futile efforts.[6]

7. PLACEMENT OFFICERS APPRAISE LIFE INSURANCE RECRUITING

a. *Caliber of the Recruiter*

The Director of Placement of a leading New England institution writes:

...the strength or weakness of most recruiting programs, not only in insurance but all fields of business activities, is found in the personality of the recruiter. I have found that, in general, most programs have been thoughtfully prepared and have been built for the specific company, industry, and function. Whether or not they go over then becomes largely the approach, manner and presentation of the recruiter, and his personality as well. Students, particularly seniors, who have become rather educated listeners through their college program, frequently judge a company through the personality of the recruiter, who is for them the company. For that reason, I believe it of utmost importance that any company send out strong, able, and personable individuals.[7]

The placement officers were asked to appraise the caliber of life insurance company recruiters. Of 53 who ventured an opinion, 42 indicated that their caliber is at least as high as, if not higher than, recruiters from other branches of industry; 5 noted a wide range in the ability of the recruiter; and 6 expressed a low opinion of life insurance company recruiters. One placement officer wrote, "Almost without exception, these are experienced personnel men—tactful, obliging, and not over-anxious in their dealing with seniors." And another characterized the life insurance company recruiter as "a very high type man—generally the extrovert type, easy of manner, friendly, personable." On the other hand, the placement officer of a midwest university replied:

In general [they are] below the caliber of [men] recruiting from other fields of business. Although most of them are very enthusiastic about the life insurance industry, they know so little about personnel work and the functions of interviewing that they discourage graduates from entering the field.

6. *Ibid.*

7. Response to Questionnaire for College and University Placement Directors (see Appendix II).

Whenever a respondent differentiated between the home office and the field recruiter, he had a good word for the home office man to the disadvantage of the branch manager or general agent. Said one, "Most men from home office—very good. Some men from agencies—very good to excellent; others—impossible!"

Several mentioned a tendency for life insurance recruiters to "oversell" both students and placement officer on the advantages of a life insurance career. One officer expressed his opinion of such recruiters thus:

> Some are too aggressive and believe we should "sell" applicants on Life Insurance as a career. We believe college placement offices should furnish material but should use no pressure in behalf of any industry.

There is every indication that such remarks are directed toward recruiters for sales rather than for non-sales positions.

b. *Outstanding Examples of Recruiting Technique*

The placement officers were asked if they cared to describe any outstandingly good or bad examples of life insurance company recruiting technique for home office positions. One company was cited as doing "one of the best jobs on any campus." This is because it sends literature which describes the company and employment opportunities to the placement director in sufficient time for him to distribute it to interested students. Furthermore, the recruiter is a trained personnel specialist who can talk with authority on any position in the company.

Several bad examples were mentioned. But, again, despite the attempt to limit the replies to home office recruiting by the wording of the question, it is obvious that these answers refer to the recruiting of sales personnel. For example, one placement officer recalls:

> One man obtained through a secretary the names of the men in our graduating class and then sent each a personal letter saying I had referred him to the student. In some cases these letters went to students who had asked not to be contacted re insurance. Needless to say, I was bitter.

This is significant in that the blunders made by non-trained field recruiters tend to remain in the minds of the placement officers and to color their attitude toward life insurance in general. Over and over again the placement officers stressed the necessity that the life insurance recruiter be a professional personnel man if he is to compete with the highly competent representatives of leading industrial concerns.

c. *Recruiting Literature*

Almost invariably, those firms which have made the best record in college recruitment publish literature designed to acquaint the students with employment opportunities offered in their company. The life insurance companies were polled in order to see how many have developed literature expressly designed to recruit college graduates for home office employment. Of 57 companies which gave this information, only 7 have prepared such literature; another 3 reported that it is in the process of preparation. All of the companies issuing this literature are large, but not necessarily giant, companies; one has only 400 home office employees. Many additional companies publish literature written to recruit agents on the campus; others distribute employee handbooks and annual reports to policyholders. But these are of limited usefulness as recruiting aids for home office positions.

As is the case with most recruiting literature used by industry, the life insurance company publications prepared to attract the college graduate toward a career in the home office put primary emphasis on the opportunities available to the graduate. Each of the booklets is objective in tone and in no sense attempts a high-pressure selling job on the superiority of the company, its product, or its opportunities. The titles of six of the booklets which have been examined indicate their orientation to the graduate's point of view; "Your Future with the ———," "Opportunity and Security with the ———," "The College Man and ———," "Opportunities for College Men," "Opportunities for College Women," "An Opportunity in Management."

Most of these booklets are brief and range in size from only 3 pages to 26. The majority are attractively printed on glossy paper, and some are profusely illustrated. In addition to the booklet outlining the employment opportunities in general terms, several of the companies distribute mimeographed sheets once or twice a year which describe more specifically current job openings and indicate starting salaries and educational qualifications required. One booklet has a pocket built in it for the insertion of this mimeographed material. Placement officers interviewed have generally applauded the brevity of these publications, feeling that the graduating senior has neither the time nor inclination to read through voluminous recruiting literature. They emphasized, too, the desirability of providing information which the students may take with them for study at their leisure, rather than one elaborate publication which can be seen only in the placement office.

The recruiting booklet typically begins with a brief history and description of the company itself. This section usually points up the distinctive characteristics of the company—perhaps its rate of growth, dominant size in the industry, pioneering activities, or the quality of service performed for policyholders. One company devotes three pages to the history and development of life insurance in general. Prominent in most of these introductory statements is an assertion of the stability of the business, with the resultant job security offered in the life insurance home office.

The bulk of the pamphlets is devoted to more or less detailed descriptions of the positions available in the various sections of the company. For example, one such booklet devotes about a page each to the accident department, the actuarial department, the agency department, the claim department, the comptroller's department, the group departments, the investment departments, the life underwriting department, the office services department, the personnel and planning department, and the reinsurance department. Another booklet divides each job description into three sections, headed: "What does a [e.g.] Methods Analyst do?", "What qualifications are desired?", "What training does the position offer?"

One of the booklets largely consists of a description of the training offered by the company. This brochure differs from the others in that it describes a management training program developed in one division of the company, rather than company-wide employment opportunities. Each phase of the formal training program is discussed in detail, illustrated by photographs depicting the teaching techniques employed. After the section on training, the paths of advancement open to graduates of the training program are outlined.

Two of the companies have prepared material designed especially to attract college women. One multi-line organization has a companion booklet to its "Opportunities for College Men" entitled "Opportunities for College Women." It describes the qualifications desired, the training offered, and the nature of the work in actuarial science, insurance underwriting, group insurance, forms analysis, and statistical administration. The other company issues a mimeographed statement of job opportunities, salary offered, and working conditions for women. This statement emphasizes opportunities in public relations and advertising, cost allocation, actuarial work, and methods and planning.

The placement officers polled generally expressed approval of the literature specifically designed for home office recruitment. The following comments, for example, were typical:

> In general the literature has been satisfactory. We receive booklets on the industry as well as booklets from individual companies. The quality and content of such booklets is generally superior to other industries.

> Generally on a par with the better materials from other companies recruiting college graduates.

Of 47 placement directors commenting on the literature, 34 indicated approval, whereas 13 were critical. Many of those who approved expressed disappointment over the fact that very few companies distribute literature. As one officer puts it:

> For the most part, [the literature is] well done by the major companies who are really interested in doing a good job and have been doing it for some time. Many have done very little on a formal basis so literature is weak.

What are the criticisms? Several report that the booklets are too long. On the other hand, some feel there is not enough material in them. One placement man writes:

> They give no idea of the kind of work which would be done in insurance firms. There are no typical job descriptions; they say nothing about interesting work that offers a challenge; they are generalized with words like "opportunity," "security," "interesting work," etc. They read like an advertisement instead of a recruiting pamphlet.

It must be noted, however, that neither the indictment of excess length nor that of excessive generality appears to be applicable to the literature just described. Perhaps these placement people refer to literature other than that specifically designed for home office recruitment. Another officer takes exception to the emphasis on security found in some of the pamphlets: "Most have an 'old' look. Usually emphasis is placed on stability rather than chances for advancement. This is not so important to college graduates as are the advancement possibilities." The booklets examined do not devote much space to the insurance industry in general. A few placement officers criticized this. One believes the literature "should have more original contact appeal to attract the man who is somewhat uninformed of insurance." Other officers have commended the material on the industry as a whole as published by the Institute of Life Insurance, the Life Insurance Agency Management Association, and other such groups. No doubt the individual companies have relied on such publications to provide a general introduction to the field.

While several placement officers approve of the objective and judicious manner in which employment opportunities are presented, this has raised some objection in other quarters. For example, one officer wrote, "For some reason most of our good men shy away from insurance—both sales and home office. Could it be that the descriptive literature doesn't show enough 'oomph' in insurance?" The placement officer of a leading "Ivy League" institution feels, on the other hand, that "oomph" is too frequently overdone in recruiting literature throughout industry. He asserts that too many fancy brochures are written by the advertising department rather than by those responsible for training and placement. He points out that the placement officer, as well as the student, reads the literature and is unfavorably impressed by too glowing a picture. As he puts it, "the college man is a little cold to people looking into the sunset."

8. EMPLOYEES APPRAISE LIFE INSURANCE RECRUITING

The college-level home office employees interviewed were asked to comment upon the college recruiting activity of their companies. Employees of those companies which do not have an active recruiting program generally feel that such a program would be desirable, although several noted that there is only a limited number of positions available which would appeal to college graduates. One man stated that there had been three openings in the investment department for many months, but that the personnel department, which does not send representatives to the campus, failed to fill them. He could not see how this department expected three individuals to walk in and ask for appointments as trainees for security analysts' positions. In this case, members of the investment department went to campuses and secured the men themselves.

Seven of the nine companies in which employees were interviewed carry on active college recruiting programs and these employees were, on the whole, uncritical of their techniques. Several of the more experienced employees believe that their companies should not wait until the senior year to begin recruiting college people. They suggest more widespread use of summer employment between the junior and senior year, or even after the sophomore year. It was suggested, too, that more emphasis be placed on cultivating teachers of insurance, since they may have more influence on the student in directing him toward an insurance career than the placement officers. Several actuarial students who revealed that they had only the vaguest idea of the functions of an actuary while undergraduates feel that more information on this career should be made available to mathematics majors early in their college course.

❋ Selection ❋

Highlights of Chapter 5

Personnel officials of companies which actively engage in college recruiting consider such criteria of selection as creative ability, initiative, resourcefulness, and dependability, in addition to intelligence.

"Ability to get along with others" is considered by college-level home office personnel to be the most important qualification of a successful home office employee. They believe, also, that an individual must be relatively stable and mature in order to be patient with comparatively slow advancement during the first few years.

Company officials place little importance on the specific course of study pursued by applicants for employment in most life insurance companies. More home office employees are hired from colleges of business administration than from liberal arts colleges, but many personnel officials express a strong preference for graduates of good liberal arts colleges.

College courses in insurance are not considered essential for the prospective home office employee, but "they are nice to have."

Companies with highly organized college recruiting programs have established selection processes involving interviews and screening tests on the campus and at the home office, to which promising applicants are invited at company expense.

Considerably more reliance is placed on interviews than on test results; few personnel officials hire or reject on test scores alone.

✻ *Chapter Five* ✻

SELECTION

CAREFUL selection of college-trained applicants for employment is of utmost importance if they are to be successfully inducted into the home office. As noted previously, proper screening is considered by company officers to be the key to harmonious relations between college trainees and other employees. Those likely to become quickly dissatisfied with less than meteoric advances in salary and responsibility can be detected and eliminated in the screening process, thus minimizing the principal problem involved in working with young college graduates. And of course it is necessary to select only those who regard a home office career as interesting and challenging and who have the capacity to fill the administrative and technical positions which it is expected they will eventually attain.

The first inquiries in this chapter concern the kind of college graduates the life insurance companies are trying to obtain. What personal qualities are sought? What educational requirements have been established? In this connection, the relative preference for liberal arts and business administration graduates is discussed, as is the desirability of college courses in insurance prior to employment with the insurance company. The special college training desired for actuarial candidates is also considered. Finally, the selection techniques employed by the leaders in the college recruiting field are surveyed.

1. PERSONAL QUALITIES SOUGHT BY INSURANCE COMPANIES

Those companies which hire substantial numbers of college trained individuals on an organized basis have summed up the qualifications desired in this type of employee.

In order to develop specifications for the individuals it wishes to obtain, one company drew up job analyses for each of the positions for which college graduates would be hired. The analyses revealed three basic types of positions:

> The first included all those jobs involving responsibility for the planning and organizing, and control of the flow, of work through various different divisions of the Company, that is, jobs involving supervision.
>
> The second group were those jobs involving the application of critical analysis and judgment to individual problems, and the formation of decisions and recommendations on courses of action to be followed: such as claim examiners, life underwriters, mortgage loan underwriters, and stock and bond analysts.
>
> In the third general classification were those jobs concerned with sales and sales management activities including the more technical type of selling in the Group insurance field.[1]

Although the relative importance of different personal qualities varies, depending upon the type of position, officers of this company feel it important to predetermine such factors as:

> ...mental abilities; mental alertness, numerical facility, verbal facility, creative ability and general organizing and planning abilities; performance factors such as initiative, resourcefulness, dependability, follow-through, etc.; background factors, including the effects of environment and early home training on the development of the individual; present social adjustment which includes an appraisal of the individual's outside activities and interests; a general over-all impression, which covers the applicant's appearance, speech, manner, neatness and so forth; and personality factors such as cooperativeness, sense of humor, interest drives, maturity, poise and social sensitivity.[2]

Officials of another company which has a well-established college recruiting program have developed a list of qualities sought in the selection of trainees. They feel that the possession of these qualities distinguishes the trainee from the ordinary employee and marks the potential executive. The list is reproduced below:

1. Accepts and looks for responsibility.
2. Relates own goals to company objectives—can put company needs ahead of his own.

1. Philip H. Yost, "Selection and Development of Personnel for Technical and Supervisory Positions," *Proceedings of the 1946 Special Conference, Life Office Management Association* (New York: L.O.M.A., 1948), p. 236.

2. *Ibid.*

3. Follows up, is dependable and conscientious—can be counted on. Thorough.
4. Has a good mind in the sense that he learns readily. Grasps new ideas. Able to organize and plan.
5. Can take discouragement—can persevere, take pressure and discipline.
6. Can evaluate own limitations in handling a situation.
7. People like him and enjoy working with him. He commands their respect. Meets them easily.
8. Has good ethical make-up—character above reproach. Has courage of his own convictions and can stick to his guns.
9. Has good facility in expressing himself both orally and in writing.
10. Is enthusiastic about what he does. Gets a kick out of his work.
11. Uses imagination—looks beyond immediate problem. Can think creatively or constructively. Has a positive outlook.
12. Has energy and purpose in what he does and performs consistently and uniformly. A hard worker. Keeps busy in an organized way.
13. Has balance, discretion, and a sense of humor about situations and people.
14. Sets high, self-imposed standards for his accomplishment—is self-critical—has pride in performance.
15. Is ambitious—looks for ways of improving his qualifications.
16. Has good capacity to think and act on his own initiative. Is good at pulling facts together and evaluating them to make decisions.
17. Adapts readily to changing work situations—can think on his feet.
18. Meets or exceeds customary standards in grooming and appearance.

The college-level home office employees who were interviewed were asked what personal qualities they would seek if they were responsible for the selection of college graduates for home office positions.

They pointed out that the qualifications depend to a large extent on the particular job the individual would be called upon to perform, but were almost unanimous in placing "ability to get along with others" at the very top of the list of general qualifications. As many indicated, this ability is even more important than skill in handling involved technical problems, even for actuaries. On the other hand, the extremely extroverted, "back-slapping" sales personality, it is agreed, would become impatient with the amount of detail work most home office positions require, and would be better suited to insurance sales work. "Original sparkle," said one man, "is not nearly as important as the ability to wear well."

They would also seek stable, mature individuals, who would be patient with relatively slow advancement in the first few years, valuing the security and low-pressure nature of the home office work above spectacular financial success. A number of those interviewed suggested that the applicant be married or contemplating marriage in the near future, because family responsibilities exert a stabilizing influence on the young man. Others doubt, however, whether the salaries offered during the first few years are adequate to support a wife and children.

Few of those interviewed would seek out "high-powered intellects" for home office employment, except for actuarial training. As long as an individual has made an adequate record in college, a congenial personality is considered more important than excellent grades. Some criticized their companies for obtaining individuals of too high caliber for the opportunities available. Such individuals fail to find the work a challenge to their capacity, and quit. Another believes, however, that his company should hire the best men available and then do everything in its power to keep them satisfied.

2. EDUCATIONAL REQUIREMENTS

What educational requirements do life insurance companies demand of those inexperienced college graduates they hire?

Placement officers generally report that life insurance recruiters are somewhat unique in that they are willing to interview graduates who have pursued almost any course of study. This is particularly true of the larger life companies which undertake to give the new employee any necessary training themselves. These companies, too, have so many diversified employment opportunities that they can accommodate a wide variety of talents.

a. *Liberal Arts vs. Business Administration*

The companies were asked whether they have tended to hire more graduates of liberal arts colleges or of schools of business administration. Of 50 companies providing this information, 28 reported that a greater number were hired from business administration schools, while 17 obtained more from liberal arts colleges. The remaining 5 indicated a more or less even split between the two groups.

There seem to be some regional patterns of preference in this regard. In New England, which abounds with good liberal arts colleges, most of the company personnel officers interviewed on this study are products of these schools themselves and tend to favor liberal arts graduates for most positions. One New England company personnel officer feels that the business administration undergraduate tends to be too limited in outlook, that while he may make a good technician he is unlikely to be executive material. Another New Englander declared, however, that although a liberal arts graduate who majored in English, economics, history, or philosophy will be just as acceptable initially as a business administration graduate (even one who has concentrated on insurance), the good business administration student will make more progress than the liberal arts student in the long run.

Those companies polled in the Southeast also report hiring more liberal arts than business administration graduates; but there appears to be an overwhelming preference for the latter group in the West. Since a large number of the smaller companies hire college graduates from local institutions only, it may well be that such companies hire from whichever type of institution happens to be located nearby.

One placement officer observed that, while many company recruiters announce they prefer people with a wide liberal arts background, they actually hire a greater number of business administration graduates from her institution. She ascribes this paradox to the fact that business administration graduates have developed a business vocabulary which makes them appear more impressive in an interview than liberal arts graduates. Also, at her institution the typical business administration student is, she feels, of somewhat higher caliber than the typical liberal arts enrollee.

Several personnel officers noted a wide variation in quality of the products of both types of institutions. They are pleased with graduates of the top-ranking liberal arts colleges, as well as with those of the leading business administration schools, provided the latter have been to some degree exposed to the humanities. The ideal background, in the opinion of some, is a liberal arts undergraduate program followed by graduate work in business administration. Some personnel people fear, however, that a man with this background may be "too hot to handle" in that he will be hard to satisfy with less than extremely rapid progress with the company, and will turn to other employment.

The companies were asked to indicate those positions for which they prefer people with undergraduate training in liberal arts or business administration, and those for which they prefer holders of master's degrees in business administration. Obviously business administration students are preferred for accounting and investments, but with this exception it is difficult to discern any clear-cut pattern from the replies received. The greatest demand for masters in business administration is in the field of investment analysis. Table 26 summarizes the educational preferences expressed by company officers.

TABLE 26

HOME OFFICE POSITIONS FOR WHICH LIFE INSURANCE COMPANIES PREFER LIBERAL ARTS TRAINING, UNDERGRADUATE BUSINESS ADMINISTRATION TRAINING, AND GRADUATE BUSINESS ADMINISTRATION TRAINING

Position	Number of Companies Reporting
Undergraduate Liberal Arts	
Underwriting	5
Claims	5
Actuarial	4
Agency service	2
Personnel	1
Public relations	1
Policyholders' service	1
Advertising	1
Policy contract drafting	1
Supervisory	1
Correspondence	1
"All but actuarial and securities"	1
"All but accounting, statistical, or specialized fields"	2
All positions	1
Undergraduate Business Administration	
Accounting and auditing	19
Investments	6
Personnel	4
All positions	5
Administration	3
Claims	3

Underwriting	2
Office management	2
Purchasing	2
Statistics	2
Planning	1
Methods	1
Mortgage analysis	1
Agency department	1
Mortgage loan representative	1
Group representative	1
Graduate Business Administration	
Investments	7
Accounting	5
Statistics	2
Supervisory	2
Actuarial	2
Agency	1
Claims	1
Mortgage analysis	1
Personnel	1
Group administration	1
Underwriting	1
All positions	1

Source: Questionnaires sent to life insurance company officers (see Appendix I) and interviews.

b. *College Courses in Insurance*

Do life insurance companies feel that candidates for employment in home office positions should have had college training in insurance?

The general opinion on this subject as gathered from interviews and the questionnaire seems to be: "Courses in insurance are not essential, but they're nice to have." Company officers were asked if they feel the completion, prior to employment, of a college course in life insurance is "necessary," "highly desirable," "desirable," "of little importance," or "undesirable." Of 50 officers expressing an opinion, only 2 consider a previous course in life insurance to be "necessary." Fifteen consider such a course to be "highly desirable," and 26 rate it as "desirable." Officials of 7 companies, on the other hand, feel that such a course is of "little importance." The officers were also polled on the necessity or desirability of completing a course in general insurance prior to employment. Again, the largest number, 30 out of 44 replying, consider it "desirable." Only 1 officer thinks it "necessary"; 2 consider it "highly desirable"; 11 feel it to be of "little importance."

Officers of smaller companies tend to consider previous study of insurance more valuable than do officers of larger organizations. The president of a small company declared in an interview that it is too heavy a burden on such companies to support the "raw product" without previous insurance training for the number of years required to train him sufficiently to be a productive employee. He stated that his company would recruit new college graduates more actively if they received more college training in life insurance. His company subscribes to the S. S. Huebner Foundation, which provides fellowships to encourage the development of more college and university teachers of insurance. It also cooperates with a local liberal arts college in the sponsorship of classes preparing for the first ten Life Office Management Association examinations. A top executive of another small company expressed himself in similar terms. In contrast to those officers who look to the college to provide broad background only, he feels that colleges should offer more specialized courses in insurance—as technical, for example, as life insurance underwriting—in order to shift the responsibility for this training from the company to the university.

Officials of larger companies do not agree with this point of view. They feel that the inexperienced college graduate can acquire background in insurance through courses leading to the designation of Fellow of the Life Office Management Association Institute, or of Chartered Life Underwriter. New college graduates are encouraged to take such courses after their regular hours of employment. Training in technical life insurance procedures, these officials believe, should be left to the companies because each organization handles them in a different way. An officer of a large company did point out one respect in which a college course is useful, namely, that it serves to "whet the student's appetite" for insurance or to discourage him from entering the field. An individual who has had college work in insurance is likely to be more certain than someone with no background in this subject that an insurance career is suitable for him.

It will be recalled, too, that several college-level home office employees indicated that a previous course in insurance would have been valuable in introducing them to insurance terminology, which otherwise takes a rather long time to acquire.

c. *Education for Actuarial Trainees*

Several universities in this country and in Canada offer special programs for actuarial candidates. Interviews with officers in charge of actuarial training in several large Eastern companies revealed that they generally prefer the graduate of a good liberal arts college to the product of a university offering actuarial courses, even though many of the latter group will have passed three of the eight actuarial examinations before applying for employment. They find that most of the applicants from these universities have confined their studies too narrowly to actuarial science and therefore do not possess sufficiently broad background to become officers of the company. The practicing actuarial officer, they contend, spends little of his time in mathematical computation, since most of his duties are administrative.

On the other hand, it is difficult to find suitable candidates from liberal arts colleges, since the major in mathematics is likely to be interested in pure mathematics to exclusion of most other areas. The actuaries report that mathematics professors tend to encourage their most promising students to do graduate work leading to careers in teaching or research, and these men are thus lost to the actuarial field.

The ideal actuarial candidate, as these officers picture him, is a man (two of the officers interviewed are particularly anxious to employ women who seek careers as actuaries) who has a sufficient background in mathematics to pass the first four examinations given by the Society of Actuaries but who is primarily a well-rounded individual with a good training in the social sciences and the humanities. They would be particularly happy to employ one who added graduate work in business administration to his undergraduate liberal arts education. The mathematical requirements are more modest than the layman generally believes. Study of mathematics through calculus, differential equations, and higher algebra is sufficient preparation for specialized work in actuarial science.

The preference among Eastern actuaries for liberal arts graduates to graduates of universities offering actuarial courses is by no means universal. The officers responding to the questionnaire were asked to indicate whether they obtained a larger number of actuarial trainees from universities offering actuarial courses than from liberal arts colleges. Of 43 companies replying, 24 reported obtaining a greater number from universities offering actuarial courses, 15 obtained a greater number from liberal arts colleges, and 4 noted an even split between the two sources. Of course, the fact that a company obtains more trainees from one source than from another does not necessarily imply that those trainees are preferable; graduates of universities offering actuarial courses may be more readily available for actuarial training than graduates of liberal arts colleges. Undergraduate colleges of business administration, it may be noted parenthetically, are a poor source of candidates, since few of their graduates have studied mathematics beyond college algebra.

3. SELECTION PROCEDURES

As would be expected, those companies which hire a new college graduate only sporadically, when a vacancy in a specific department arises, have not developed formal selection procedures. Generally, preliminary screening is undertaken in the personnel department. The successful applicant is then interviewed by the appropriate division supervisor and probably by a department head before a final decision to employ him is made. Those companies which have established a formal recruiting and training program have developed a more or less elaborate selection procedure.

Several companies have instituted a selection process involving a series of interviews and screening tests, both on the campus and at the home office. In one such process, a preliminary interview is held on the campus by the official in charge of recruitment, and successful applicants are invited to the home office at company expense for two days of screening. The first day is devoted to a battery of screening tests and an extensive conversational interview which may take as long as two hours. The second day is given over to interviews with departmental officers and supervisors in the area where the candidate is likely to be placed. The applicant is also interviewed by an officer outside this department in order to obtain a check on his general desirability. Finally, a senior officer of the company interviews the applicant. The officer is provided with the rating forms completed by his subordinates and, if he concurs in their favorable decision, he will offer a position to the candidate. An effort is made to inform all unsuccessful candidates immediately as to the reasons for their rejection and to suggest other fields more suitable to their talents.

Two property and casualty companies have established a selection process which is deliberately designed to weed out all but the most persevering, on the assumption that only those who cannot be discouraged from a career in insurance will stick with the company long enough to repay a heavy investment in their training. Under one such procedure, the applicant who has passed a preliminary campus screening interview must undertake an elaborate, time-consuming investigation of the insurance business and of the company's place in the industry. Information is to be obtained from competing companies, insurance professors, financiers, and business men. Commenting on this investigation as a screening device, its originator states:

> The job-hunter resents it as time-consuming and an imposition on the part of the company. The career man welcomes it because he knows the company is just as interested as he is in his making the correct decision. He sees the wisdom of the suggestion that he make inquiries of or even seek employment with competing companies. He is intelligent enough to realize the company is taking the chance of losing him to a competitor, but at the same time would rather have it happen, if it is to happen, before, rather than after, training.[3]

Having completed the investigation, the candidate is brought at company expense to the home office, where he takes a physical examination and is interviewed by members of the Education and Male Employment staff. He is then subjected to four and a half hours of aptitude and interest testing, after which he is interviewed by officers representing the fire, marine, and casualty divisions of the company. Finally, the survivors go before a board of six company officers:

> At this stage little doubt remains concerning the candidates' abilities. The purpose of the committee is to study salesmanship under pressure, long-range stability and the degree of conviction and understanding achieved. Definite efforts are made to eliminate any misconceptions or misunderstandings which may have been picked up during screening. Much verbal cold water is poured so as to see if the young men are really ready for a vigorous training program and slow initial advancement. It is amazing how heretofore undiscovered attitudes crop up and how some of the best "freeze" under pressure. Positive efforts are made to be sure that candidates have not been "oversold" by anyone along the line. The obligation to remain long enough with the company to give a fair return upon a sizable training investment is emphasized and

3. H. Paul Abbott, "After Training, What Then?" (address before members of senior class, Princeton University, Dec. 8, 1948).

decision is made as to where the orientation or probationary periods of employment will be spent.[4]

An elaborate selection process is quite laborious and expensive, but it is generally considered to be worthwhile if the company contemplates investing a substantial sum in the training of the inexperienced college graduate. One large company which has had a college training program in effect for a number of decades estimates that it is necessary to interview 16 men to get one on the job. Another company interviewed 1,700 in 1950 and hired 66—about 24 men interviewed to one hired. Still another interviewed 138 graduates on the campus in order to hire one man in 1952. This company hired 4 out of 177 replying to advertisements—a 44 to 1 ratio—and hired 1 out of 43 candidates referred by employment agencies.

a. *Screening Tests*

Many companies administer one or more mental level, aptitude, interest, or personality tests as an aid in screening college-level applicants for employment. Twenty-nine of the companies polled reported the use of aptitude tests; 17 employ mental level tests; 11 use some kind of personality test; and 9, an interest test. Fifteen of the 58 companies providing this information do not make use of any screening tests.

The companies were asked to name those tests they use. Most frequently mentioned is the Life Office Management Association Examination in Clerical Work. About one-third of the companies polled make use of this test for all new "white collar" employees, regardless of their educational level or the position for which they are applying. This test measures speed and accuracy in such skills as arithmetic, verbal and numerical detail work, vocabulary, reading comprehension, and spelling. Several personnel people report that they have established a company norm, and will refuse employment to those making less than this score. At least one company which maintains a highly successful formal college recruiting program administers this test to its college trainees. The personnel director has found that the successful trainee will score above 170, while less satisfactory trainees usually score below this mark. He therefore considers it useful, even though the skills tested are largely clerical.

4. H. Paul Abbott, "Dealing in Futures" (paper presented before Insurance Educational Directors' Conference, Insurance Institute of America, New York, N.Y., June 21, 1949).

A wide variety of other tests is employed. Several companies have developed their own. Table 27 lists the tests mentioned and indicates the frequency of their use.

TABLE 27

TESTS USED BY LIFE INSURANCE COMPANIES AS AN AID IN SCREENING COLLEGE GRADUATES FOR HOME OFFICE POSITIONS

Name of Test	Number of Companies Using
Life Office Management Association Examination in Clerical Work	19
Wonderlic Personnel Test	5
Kuder Preference Record	4
American Council on Education Test of Mental Abilities	4
Clark Activity Vector Analysis	3
Strong Vocational Interest Blank	2
Thurstone Temperament Schedule	2
Bernreuter Personality Inventory	2
Allport-Vernon Scale of Values	2
Moss-Hunt Social Intelligence Test	1

Actuarial trainees are often given a mathematical aptitude test designed by the actuary in charge of their selection and training.

Several companies make use of an extensive battery of tests in order to develop a profile chart of test performance for each candidate which can be compared with those of successful employees of the company. To indicate the nature of such an elaborate testing process, a "report of test performance" as used by one company is reproduced on page 114.

Personnel officials of 18 companies indicated that they have made validity checks on the screening tests they use; 11 have not made such checks, and no information was forthcoming from the remainder of the sample of 65. In one company a study is being made with the object of reducing the number of tests used. This study has found some correlation between test results and future success on the job as indicated by merit ratings, but the correlation is not especially close. Most significant results have been obtained from the Allport-Vernon Scale of Values and the American Council on Education Mental Abilities Test. Executives of two other large companies are most impressed by the value of the Clark Activity Vector Analysis, a measure of "activity level." One officer indicated that whenever the results of this test were disregarded, "we fell on our face."

LEADERSHIP FOR LIFE INSURANCE

REPORT OF TEST PERFORMANCE

Name:____________________ Date:____________

	Standard Nine Profile								
Tests	1	2	3	4	5	6	7	8	9
1. Vocabulary									
2. Arithmetic									
3. A.C.E.:									
a. Linguistic									
b. Quantitative									
4. English Usage									
5. Paragraph Comp.									
6. Personnel Relations *									
7. Kuder:									
a. Mechanical									
b. Computational									
c. Scientific									
d. Persuasive									
e. Artistic									
f. Literary									
g. Musical									
h. Social Service									
i. Clerical									
8. Study of Values:									
a. Theoretical									
b. Economic									
c. Aesthetic									
d. Social									
e. Political									
f. Religious									

SS3632

* The Personnel Relations test has been "tailor made" for this company's special use. The other tests are widely used elsewhere.

b. *Interview Techniques*

All the personnel officials interviewed stressed that scores on screening tests are never the sole criteria for hiring or rejecting an applicant. One officer estimates that the battery of tests he employs gives information on less than a third of the factors he attempts to predetermine before hiring a college graduate. The most important part of the selection process is a series of interviews. These are indispensable in revealing the majority of the critical factors.

Considerable attention has been given by some personnel officers to the problem of developing the most efficient interview procedure. In companies where college recruiting is on a formal, continuing basis, interview rating forms have been developed. A typical form is reproduced below.

Interviewer ____________________

INTERVIEW RATING FORM

Name ______________________ Date ______________________

Age ______________ Place ______________________

A. CIVILIAN AND MILITARY WORK HISTORY

	Below Average	Average	Above Average
1. Duties?			
Civilian?			
Military?			
2. Number of previous jobs?			
3. Work involved contact with people?			
4. Likes and dislikes?			
5. How closely supervised?			
6. Working conditions?			
Long hours?			
7. Level of earnings?			
8. Any leadership experience?			
9. Reasons for changing jobs?			
10. Reasons for seeking a job with ________________			

B. EDUCATIONAL HISTORY

	Below Average	Average	Above Average
1. Best—poorest subjects?			
2. Honors—activities?			
Level of school grades?			
3. If non-grad, reason for leaving college?			
4. Training since leaving school?			
Military training?			
5. How education financed?			

C. EARLY HOME BACKGROUND

	Below Average	Average	Above Average
1. Father's occupation?			
2. Childhood factors?			
Number of brothers and sisters?			
Over-protective parents?			
Upbringing lax or strict?			
Parental guidance?			
3. Earliest age *partially* or *wholly* financially independent?			

D. PRESENT SOCIAL ADJUSTMENT

	Below Average	Average	Above Average
1. Age?			
2. Marital Status?			
3. Dependents (Number and ages)?			
4. Financial stability?			
Housing?			
Life Insurance owned?			
In debt?			
5. Recreation and interests?			
Outdoor vs. indoor?			
Groups and organizations?			
6. Wife's attitude toward insurance job?			
7. Health history?			

E. MANNER AND APPEARANCE

	Below Average	Average	Above Average
1. Personal appearance?			
Height?			
Grooming, hygiene?			
2. Speaking voice?			
3. Unfavorable mannerisms?			
4. Physical vigor?			

F. PERSONALITY QUALIFICATIONS

	Below Average	Average	Above Average
1. Emotionally mature?			
2. Self-confident?			
3. Unobtrusively aggressive?			
4. Adaptable?			
5. Social sensitivity?			
6. Extroverted vs. introverted?			
7. Economic drive?			
8. Political drive?			
9. Sense of humor?			
10. Sense of responsibility?			
11. Sincerity and honesty?			

G. SUMMARY

OVER-ALL RATING: ______Above Average
______Average
______Below Average

One company has found it desirable to prepare an interview manual for the guidance of personnel people, line supervisors, and branch managers who may be called upon to interview college level applicants. This manual is particularly useful in suggesting to the interviewer how to ascertain certain personality characteristics which are considered important to predetermine, but which may not be readily apparent. These include such factors as stability, industry, cooperation, self-reliance, maturity, perservance, competitiveness, loyalty, leadership, insight-imagination-originality, forcefulness, judgment, motivation, and capacity to grow.

The following excerpts from this manual define a few of these characteristics and the suggested means of determining them from observation and from the candidate's past history:

What to Look for.	Where to Find It.
1. STABILITY:	
Consistency of performance and activities toward pre-determined goals; firmness of character and purpose; steadiness.	Evidence of job tenure; i.e., either stayed long enough to gain real values and left, for justifiable reasons, to progress; or did not stay too long to get in a rut, lose initiative, become a drone; acquisition and

ownership of property, savings accounts, etc.; sustained interest and acquisition of skill in two or three hobbies, rather than a fleeting interest in many; has roots in community, takes active responsibility and part in group and community activities.

7. COMPETITIVENESS:

Drive, initiative, tries to outdo self and others; pride in accomplishment, active in competitive activities; more interest in opportunity than security.

Direct Observation: observation of how individual handles himself and what his attitudes are reveals his self-confidence, where he has pride in accomplishment, his willingness to "gamble" on himself.
Schooling: enters into competition with others for scholastic honors or prizes, for offices or jobs, or in athletics.
Job History: evidence of confidence to undertake and complete tasks beyond him; won sales competitions; achieves success in more than pure routine responsibilities.
Activities: competed for office in civic, social, political or fraternal organizations.

8. LOYALTY:

Attitude towards family, friends, and associates, "identifies self" with activities and organizations, a "booster" rather than a "knocker."

This is an "insight" factor which may be only inferred from the individual's prior actions and his present attitudes. His statements, expressed attitudes and actions towards people, events or things reflect his loyalty throughout his whole life history.

❋ *Training* ❋

Highlights of Chapter 6

Placement officers agree that companies offering formal training programs are more attractive to college graduates than those which do not.

Some type of organized orientation program was provided by more than half the companies sampled in 1952. These programs usually consist of several lectures on company organization, employee benefits and duties, and the company's place in the life insurance industry. College graduates desire more extensive training than is afforded by such orientation programs alone.

Less than one third of the companies sampled maintain formal actuarial programs designed to prepare employees for the Society of Actuaries examinations. Other companies conduct such preparation on an informal basis.

Twenty-three of 60 companies reporting have established formal non-actuarial training programs. Many additional companies confine their training to preparation for L.O.M.A. examinations and/or on-the-job training.

Most formal programs were started after World War II, although some have been in existence for more than 30 years.

Several leaders in college training make use of "loop" training courses in which the new employee is given brief experience in a variety of company operations. "Loop" courses run from four weeks to one year. Several companies with extensive "loop" course experience plan to curtail the duration of the programs. Employees report that "loop" courses are most beneficial in acquainting them with personnel throughout the company.

At least one life insurance company has a straight classroom training program leading to positions in management consulting. The case method of instruction is stressed.

A few companies admit women to administrative training programs primarily designed for men. Two companies maintain extensive recruiting and training activities for young college women.

College training programs raise human relations problems with non-college personnel, but these have not caused unusual difficulty.

Turnover rates of college trainees in life insurance companies compare favorably with those in other branches of industry.

✻ *Chapter Six* ✻

TRAINING

COLLEGE graduates express a strong preference for companies which offer an organized training program. This was affirmed by 62 of the 65 placement officers polled. Why do they favor organized training?

Obviously, most college graduates are convinced of the value of education, or else they would not have gone to college. They feel that their chances of success in a particular field of business will be enhanced by thorough training.

Placement officers and company personnel people believe that a desire for security is another important reason why college graduates look for training programs. The student is somewhat afraid to plunge into the business world strictly on his own after a relatively sheltered and closely supervised educational experience. Also, the larger investment a company makes in training a new employee, the greater his job security, since the firm will lose this investment if it discharges him after only a brief period with the company.

Another consideration is the lack of knowledge on the part of most college graduates about exactly what goes on inside a life insurance company home office. Very few students come to the placement office with a burning desire for, say, a career as an underwriter. Most of them have no idea what an underwriter does. The graduate wants, therefore, to be hired as a general trainee and to be exposed to a variety of positions in order to have an intelligent basis for determining the position for which he is best suited. Perhaps the college graduate also believes that the company which has developed an organized program for recruiting and training new employees is somewhat better managed than one which lacks such a program. Superiority in this phase of its operations may also be accompanied by superiority in other phases which will affect his career with the company.

In 1946, a survey of 209 life insurance companies revealed that 45 of these organizations maintained formal training programs of one type or another for non-sales personnel.[1] Forty-four companies without their own non-sales training program reported the use of outside courses for this purpose. Of this latter group, an indeterminate number merely encouraged its employees to prepare on their own for Life Office Management Association and Actuarial Society examinations.

The 45 companies which maintained training programs offered a total of 59 courses, 44 of which were classified as general and 15 as specialized. Of the general courses, 10 were designed to orient new employees to home office rules and benefits and to the broad field of life insurance. The largest number, 24, was devoted to preparing employees for the L.O.M.A. examinations. In 5 cases, the company itself developed a course in life insurance fundamentals, and the remaining courses were given over to such miscellaneous objectives as public speaking and correspondence.

The 15 specialized courses included several of particular interest to the college graduate employed in the life insurance business. Two involved actuarial training. Two others were courses for cashiers in field offices; one of these courses also served as a general administrative training program for potential home office employees. One other course was reported to be in the general area of administrative training, a 100-hour program covering the functions of the various departments of the company.

Eight companies had, as of 1946, instituted 10-hour supervisory training courses patterned after the "Training Within Industry" Job Instruction, Job Relations, and Job Methods courses. The remaining courses involved stenography and business mathematics.

One is impressed by the small number of formal training programs which would attract the inexperienced college graduate to a career in a life insurance company home office. Undoubtedly some programs which had been in operation prior to World War II were suspended during wartime and were not reconstituted in 1946. Other companies probably maintained supervised on-the-job training for college graduates but failed to report them because they felt the 1946 survey was

1. Richard deR. Kip, *Education and Training Activities of Insurance Companies and Associations* (Philadelphia: Wharton School of Finance and Commerce, 1947), pp. 21-23.

interested in classroom courses only. But it is apparent that much of the formal training which is currently offered by life insurance companies to college graduates was inspired by the post-war need to compete with industrial firms for the services of this segment of the labor force.

In this chapter, the nature of the home office training available to college graduates in 1952 is examined. After a brief consideration of orientation programs which are not designed specifically for the college graduate, actuarial training is discussed. The bulk of the chapter is given over to an examination of non-actuarial, administrative training programs; their extent; the number of years they have been established; and the number of employees they have involved. Several examples of "loop" and classroom training as carried out in companies of different sizes are presented in some detail in order to illustrate typical curricula and methods of supervision and evaluation. This is followed by the results of a survey of placement officer opinion on the requisites of an optimum training program. Other types of programs are briefly described, including group sales and service training, programs for college women, summer and internship programs. A discussion of some of the problems in human relations evoked by the establishment of a training program then follows, and the chapter concludes with an inquiry into whether trainees typically stay with the companies long enough to repay the investment in their training.

1. ORIENTATION PROGRAMS

Orientation programs are considered valuable in making easier the induction of new college graduates into the life insurance company home office. Twenty-nine out of 47 companies providing this information in 1952 maintained some sort of formal orientation program for new employees. As might be expected, these programs are more frequently found among the large than among the small companies.

The goals of the different orientation programs are quite similar. The new employee is to be acquainted with his benefits and his responsibilities as a member of the company. He is to gain some familiarity with the functions of his company and the way in which it is organized to carry them out. He may also be given an introduction to the general subject of life insurance, its role in society, and his company's place in the life insurance industry.

Various companies devote from 2½ to 12 hours to orientation. Four or

5 hours seems to be the typical program length. In addition, one company maintains a six-month tour of all major departments in order to orient college men, and another provides one half-day of classroom instruction per week during the first year of employment for college graduates. These last-mentioned programs might better be classified as college training programs, a discussion of which follows later in this chapter.

Many of the companies have found that it is undesirable to give too extensive a program to the new employee immediately upon his arrival. One company confines a preliminary briefing to three-quarters of an hour and postpones more elaborate indoctrination until the employee has been with the company between one and two weeks. Another company holds the first session on the first day of work, the second after two weeks, the third after one month, and the fourth after six months. In addition to lectures by a member of the training staff, many companies include meetings with the president and other officers, tours of the building, and showings of filmstrips and movies.

While such orientation programs are helpful in the adjustment of the new college graduate, they obviously, with the exception of the two elaborate programs for college people mentioned above, are not what the college student contemplates when he expresses preference for companies offering formal training programs.

2. ACTUARIAL TRAINING

The college training program earliest established in most companies is for the training of actuaries. An actuarial officer is customarily made responsible for recruiting, selecting, and training a group of young college graduates, with the dual purpose of preparing them for the examinations of the Society of Actuaries and having them perform productive work in the actuarial department. In order that the broad nature of the training required for the actuarial examinations may be appreciated, the examination syllabus is outlined below:

A. Preliminary Actuarial Examinations

Part 1. Language Aptitude Examination

Part 2. General Mathematics Examination
Algebra, trigonometry, coordinate geometry, calculus.

Part 3. Special Mathematics Examination
Finite differences, probability and statistics.

B. Associateship

Part 4. Compound interest and annuities—certain, life contingencies, multiple decrement tables.

Part 5. Construction of mortality and disability tables; sources and characteristics of principal mortality and disability tables; selection of risks, including underwriting of disability and additional accidental death benefits, insurance of under-average lives and premiums for extra hazards.

C. Fellowship

Part 6. Gross premiums; valuation of liabilities of life insurance organizations; non-forfeiture values and change or reinstatement of life insurance contracts.

Part 7. Analysis and distribution of surplus; life insurance accounting; investment of life insurance funds and valuation of assets.

Part 8. Life insurance law; employee retirement plans; group insurance; social insurance; actuarial phases of agency problems.[2]

Most college students with an interest in mathematics have sufficient background to take the first two examinations. The third examination involves study of probability and finite differences, which are presented in many college courses in actuarial mathematics. It is not unusual, therefore, for a trainee to enter life insurance company employment having passed the first three examinations. He is particularly likely to have accomplished this if he has graduated from a university offering a major in actuarial science. Many actuarial trainees are hired, however, who have not yet passed the preliminary examinations.

The associateship and fellowship examinations involve subject matter which can be mastered only while the candidate is in the employ of a life insurance company. In addition to such strictly "actuarial" topics as the construction of mortality tables, the computation of premiums, and the valuation of reserves, the fellowship candidate must be conversant with underwriting, accounting, investments, law, and even certain agency problems.

A training program which is to prepare the candidate for these phases of the examinations must necessarily include observation, if not actual job experience, in many departments of the company out-

2. Adapted from Society of Actuaries, *Preliminary Actuarial Examinations* (Chicago, 1950).

side the actuarial. The examinations provide a tangible goal toward which the trainee strives, and they also tend to keep training from being sidetracked under the pressure of daily production needs.

Actuarial training programs are conducted with varying degrees of formality. Of 48 companies responding on this question, only 14 reported formal actuarial training programs in operation. Several others indicated, however, that while no formal program exists, actuarial trainees are rotated from job to job in order to get experience for the examinations; they receive help on an informal basis from senior actuarial officers, and often are allowed to study for the examinations on company time. As might be expected, the number of employees designated as actuarial trainees varies greatly from company to company. The smallest companies, having less than 250 employees, usually have no one with such a title, although one company in the 100-250 employee bracket reports as many as 7. Medium-sized organizations, with 500 to 1,000 employees, generally reported between 2 and 6 in this classification. The top ten companies in terms of size usually have 20 or 25 trainees, while one giant company employs more than 100 actuarial trainees at the present time.

Formal training programs differ somewhat from one another, but since their common objective involves preparation for the examinations, the similarities are more conspicuous than the differences. A typical program calls for 20 to 35 hours of study in addition to the regular 37½-hour work week. At this rate a trainee is expected to achieve Fellowship in from four to eight years, depending upon his ability and willingness to work. The trainee begins on routine clerical assignments within the actuarial department, and, as he learns a job, is shifted to another within the department, gradually progressing to positions requiring great technical competence and involving supervision over other employees. In one company, trainees are often assigned to special research projects, such as the development of a new premium or dividend scale, in order better to acquaint them with theoretical problems underlying day-to-day operations.

Such on-the-job training is supplemented by some formal classroom instruction, although the trainee must depend, for the most part, on his own study. One hour per day of classroom instruction, either on company time or after the work day, is frequently provided. Usually such classes are conducted by a company actuarial officer, although in some areas the local actuarial society offers cooperative classes. One company reports that it gives one hour per day instruction time for six months preceding each examination, supplemented by an additional hour per day for the month immediately preceding the examination.

Experience in other departments is obtained largely by observation under most programs surveyed, although some companies assign trainees to actual operations. A trainee may sit in with investment analysts as they pass upon applications for term loans or mortgages; he may consult with underwriters and members of the medical department in determining the statistical basis for underwriting a given risk. Several actuaries in charge of these programs have expressed regret at being unable to spare the trainees from the actuarial department long enough for them to get actual on-the-job experience in other areas.

The actuary of one company employing as many as 100 actuarial trainees at one time predicts that from 25 to 35 out of this group will eventually become Fellows of the Society of Actuaries. He reports a higher proportion of successful candidates among those hired in the earlier 'thirties because during depression years there was little competition for outstanding men from engineering firms. There is, he notes, a sharp demarcation between the person who stops at the Associateship level and the one who achieves Fellowship. A "bookworm" may become an Associate, but it requires an original thinker to obtain the higher designation. Associates who cannot make the grade serve a useful purpose in the company as competent technicians, but they cannot become actuaries. It used to be the policy in most companies to dismiss trainees upon failure of an examination. Today these individuals are generally offered positions outside the training program which are commensurate with their ability.

Successful candidates not only fill officer positions within the actuarial department, but tend to permeate the other departments of the company. For example, in one large company the vice-president in charge of group sales is an actuary, as are the controllers of the two largest companies. Several company presidents are actuaries, although there seems to be a trend toward the selection of investment or legal experts for the chief executive position.

Many successful candidates are hired away from the company which trained them by other, usually smaller, companies and, increasingly, by actuarial consulting firms. Because of the great growth of pension plans in recent years, services of the consulting actuary are in great demand, and consulting firms can entice actuaries from the life insurance companies by offering them several thousand dollars a year more in salary.

3. ADMINISTRATIVE TRAINING PROGRAMS

a. *Number Established*

An effort was made to visit most of the companies along the Eastern seaboard which have developed formal home office training programs primarily designed for new college graduates. Some of these programs are described below. The questionnaire distributed to other companies throughout the country asked:

> Has your company a formal training program (or programs) for non-actuarial home office positions? If so, please describe, indicating use of job rotation, on-the-job training, classroom instruction, home assignments, etc. Please note length of time spent on each phase.

Unfortunately, the responses to this question were, for the most part, of so general and sketchy a nature that it is difficult to report with any certainty on the number of companies which do have a "formal training program."

Many indicated on-the-job training only. Others use solely the L.O.M.A. examinations. In some companies, on-the-job training undoubtedly involves a well thought-out program designed to develop the new college graduate to his highest potential—a program in which he is given the opportunity to advance to positions requiring greater technical skill and supervisory responsibility as his performance warrants, and in which he is allowed to observe the operations of the company as a whole by intra- and inter-departmental job rotation. On the other hand, "on-the-job" training may mean nothing more than placing the college graduate in a clerical position which has to be filled at the moment.

In some companies, classes are held to prepare for the L.O.M.A. examinations; in these classes the college graduate, along with any other interested company employees, is instructed in the fundamentals of life insurance. Few companies offer classes in the more advanced phases of these examinations because of the limited number of people preparing for any one examination at any time. While preparation for the L.O.M.A. examinations undoubtedly is an excellent supplement to a training program designed expressly for the new college graduate, it is doubtful whether it can be considered a satisfactory substitute for such a program.

In order to catalog the extent of formal non-actuarial home office training for new college graduates, it was necessary to decide arbitrarily whether or not the activities described in the questionnaire responses represent a formal training program. Those programs involving the L.O.M.A. examinations alone and those confined to on-the-job training with no mention of formal supervision were eliminated from this list. Of 60 companies providing this information, 23 reported activities which qualify, in the writer's opinion, as a formal non-actuarial training program. Twelve of the 37 companies whose activities do not seem to constitute a formal training program indicated that they encourage their employees to take L.O.M.A. examinations. Many of the 23 companies with formal training programs use the L.O.M.A. program as a supplement to other activities.

b. *Year Instituted*

Most of the formal training programs are relatively new, which is the reason they were not reported in the 1946 survey mentioned above. Information on the starting dates of their programs was provided by 18 companies. Although some programs were in operation in the 1920's, the majority have been introduced since 1946. These figures are tabulated in Table 28.

TABLE 28

STARTING DATES OF 18 LIFE INSURANCE COMPANY NON-ACTUARIAL HOME OFFICE TRAINING PROGRAMS

	Number of Companies
1920-1929	3
1930-1939	1
1940-1945	0
1946	2
1947	3
1948	2
1949	1
1950	1
1951	4
1952	1
Total	18

Source: Questionnaires sent to life insurance company officers (see Appendix I) and interviews.

Compared with other lines of business, most life insurance companies have started rather late in the development of college training programs. According to a 1948 survey in which information on 142 companies in all branches of business was obtained, 18 per cent had inaugurated college training programs before 1920; 39 per cent, between 1920 and 1939; and 37 per cent have done so since 1940.[3]

c. *Number of Employees Enrolled*

The number of persons currently enrolled in a given home office training program differs widely from company to company. Only 14 companies provided this information; they reported from 1 to 51 college-level employees in training as of mid-1952. Eight companies indicated that between 1 and 8 employees were currently enrolled in a formal training program, two companies reported 12 each, and four companies reported between 20 and 51. The companies were also asked to report the number of employees trained since the beginning of the program. Here the range is from the 3 or 4 currently enrolled up to 535 trained by one giant company which instituted its program in 1920. Typically, 30 or 40 individuals have completed such a program in those companies which have had formal programs established for a number of years.

d. *Kind of Training*

There is considerable variation in the type of training offered the non-specialized college graduate. The necessity of passing the Actuarial Society examinations provides a basis of organization for actuarial training which is lacking in the non-actuarial programs. Differences in company size and lines of business written make for variation in the type of training offered, as do differences in the training philosophy adhered to by those in charge of the programs and differences in the degree of support top management gives to the training.

Those life insurance companies which have gained reputations for maintaining the best training programs make use of "loop" training, classroom training, or both. Under the "loop" program, the trainee spends a designated length of time in each of several departments in the company, actually working on-the-job in some cases and merely observing in others. Sometimes a combination of classroom training and the "loop" method is used. The trainee may spend half the day on the job

3. Stephen Habbe, *College Graduates in Industry* (New York: National Industrial Conference Board, 1948), p. 5.

and the other half in the classroom, or else several days or weeks of classroom training may be alternated with on-the-job training.

(1) *"Loop" Training*

The "loop" type of training is considered particularly useful in giving the new employee an over-all picture of the company's operations in order that he may more intelligently choose a field of specialization suitable to his aptitudes and interest, and that the job to which he is assigned will be more meaningful when he understands how it fits into the company's operations. "Loop" training tends also to overcome the excessive compartmentalization that characterizes many insurance organizations. An officer of a large company remarked that in terms of the attitudes of the employees and the specialized nature of their work, each department might just as well be a separate corporation.

(*a*) *A Small Company's Program.*—While there is more organized training activity among the large than among the small companies, the formal training program is by no means the monopoly of the giant organization. For example, one of the most thorough-going programs in effect today involves only five trainees in a West coast company which had, as of 1951, less than $60 million insurance in force.[4] In this program, the trainee group is directly under the supervision of the executive vice-president, who is responsible for the actual management of the company. A chairman of the trainee group is appointed from the members of the group for a three-month period and acts as the executive vice-president's administrative assistant in charge of trainee activities. The chairman presides at a regularly scheduled biweekly meeting of the group with the executive vice-president. Another member of the trainee group is appointed secretary for meetings of the company's officers on a rotating basis. As secretary he consults with the presiding officer in the preparation of the agenda, prepares the minutes, and distributes them to the appropriate company officials. In this way members of the trainee group may actually participate in the formulation of top level policy.

Trainees are recruited at selected colleges—the executive vice-president has personally participated in this activity—as well as from within the organization. A college degree is not a prerequisite for the program but is preferred. The training program itself begins with a week's orien-

4. See Edward B. Matthews, III, "Training for Management," Life Office Management Association Interim Report, Sept. 13-14, 1951.

tation, which involves brief visits in each department of the company and the study of a Trainee Orientation Manual. This manual briefly describes the history of the company; its functional organization; and the duties, functions and regulations of the trainee group. It also contains diagrams of the physical layout of the home office. After the orientation period, the trainee undergoes a three-phase program involving on-the-job training, academic training, and "external" training.

Fifteen months of on-the-job training has been scheduled in order that the trainee become versed in every operation in the home office. He must perform every job in a department, including that of department manager. He prepares a job description for each position he fills as well as a confidential report to the executive vice-president in which each job as well as the performance of departmental personnel is evaluated. The trainees are encouraged to submit recommendations for the improvement of methods and standards, these recommendations providing a basis for the evaluation of the trainee. A definite schedule for the rotation of each trainee from job to job during the 15 months has been worked out and is reproduced below:

Function of Department	*Time Spent*
Flow of New Business	6 weeks
Office Services Department	8 weeks
Flow of Cash	2 weeks
Collections and Disbursements Department	4 weeks
Auditing and Accounting Department	6 weeks
Policy Issue Section	2 weeks
Underwriting Department	6 weeks
Actuarial-Statistical Department	4 weeks
Policyholders Service and Claims Department	6 weeks
Group Department	6 weeks
1. Sales	2 weeks
2. Policy Issue	2 weeks
3. Claims	2 weeks
Investment Department	4 weeks
Agency Department	6 weeks
Executive Department	4 weeks

The trainee begins by studying the flow of new business through the company's home office and is then put in charge of the office services department, which has a permanent assistant department manager, while the managership is rotated among the trainees. The office services department controls the files for policies and claims, miscellaneous correspondence, and inspection service. This department also has charge of the supplies, multigraphing, addressographing, photostat work, the switchboard, and janitorial service. After two months in charge of office services, the trainee enters the technical part of his on-the-job training, spending from two to six weeks in all phases of the company's activities, including, it will be noted, the executive department. Upon completion of this schedule the trainee is permanently placed within the home office in a position mutually acceptable to the trainee and to the executive vice-president.

After permanent placement, the trainee commences the academic phases of the program. Each trainee, regardless of background, is expected to work for a Fellowship in the Life Office Management Association Institute and for the Chartered Life Underwriter designation. In addition, he must complete a home study course which was developed within the company and which covers business writing, personnel relations, economics, investments, business law, accounting, and management practices. Texts needed in order to prepare for the L.O.M.A. and C.L.U. examinations are furnished by the company, and examination fees are refunded upon successful completion of the examinations.

In the external phase of his training, the employee often spends time in other insurance companies with which reciprocal arrangements have been developed, studying their procedures and techniques in his chosen branch of insurance operations. He is also charged with the preparation of research reports involving contact with such outside organizations as the Institute of Life Insurance, L.O.M.A., the Life Insurance Agency Management Association, and the American College of Life Underwriters, as well as with organizations outside the life insurance industry. In addition, the executive vice-president may authorize him to pursue university study in some phase of insurance. A last and apparently unique requirement is for all trainees to obtain actual experience in insurance production. A minimum of $100,000 insurance written is considered necessary in order to familiarize each trainee with the problems of the field forces.

This résumé indicates the unusual degree to which the trainee under this program is exposed to all operations of the company. Apparent, too, is the close relationship between top management and trainee. The operating head of the company is, in effect, the training director. The arrangement whereby responsibility for the operation of the office services department is thrust upon the new trainee is certainly a daring test of his capacity for supervision. It seems, nonetheless, to be feasible, since technical competence in insurance operations is not necessary for running that department. Many features of the program could be carried out only in a very small company. Executives of large companies would hesitate to delegate department head functions to a member of a college training program. Other companies may also hesitate to initiate a procedure whereby the trainees submit confidential reports on departmental personnel directly to the company's chief executive, lest it arouse considerable resentment on the part of other employees.

(*b*) *A Very Large Company's Program.*—A college training program in effect in one giant company is not fundamentally different from the one just outlined for the very small company. In 1952 the former organization hired 70 new college graduates. Fifty-eight of them were assigned directly to positions in auditing, contract drafting, cost allocation, claims, methods, group, underwriting, and other departments. The remaining 12 were selected for a special home office training program, involving seven different assignments during the first year with the company. Since 1947, when the program went into effect, more than 100 individuals have been graduated from the training program. Each trainee is assigned to one or more positions within each of the following areas: underwriting, accounting, servicing of business in force, claims, group insurance, methods, and in a district office.

Written reports are not required of the trainees except by some division managers who are curious to see what the trainees have learned from the operations. An assistant personnel director in charge of male employment and training is responsible for the trainees and obtains reports on their progress from the manager of each division to which they are assigned. On page 135 a rating sheet which managers are asked to complete is reproduced. In addition, the training director has the manager indicate in a letter his observations on the trainee with respect to:

1. Ability to learn and thoroughly understand the job.
2. Attitude toward the job.
3. Ability to get along well with his associates.
4. Work habits.
5. Quality of work.
6. Quantity of work.
7. Major weaknesses.

8. Major strong points.
9. Potential capacity for future development and advancement.

MANAGER'S RATING OF HOME OFFICE TRAINEE

Person Rated ______________________ Division ______________

The purpose of the following ratings is to obtain your evaluation of how well you think the above Trainee will get along with other persons in different work situations. Assuming that he has been permanently assigned to your Division, based upon your observations, how would you feel about his being placed on each of the following types of assignments? Check the statement which best describes your feeling. Please rate him in *all* four of the assignments, even though some of them may not be relevant to work in your Division.

Assignment 1

One where appearance and manner are important in making a favorable first impression.

——enthusiastic about having him
——pleased to have him
——satisfied to have him
——accept him with reservations
——reluctant to have him
——would not want him

Comments: ______________________

____

Assignment 2

One requiring ability to get along harmoniously with others where he has no responsibility for their supervision. The majority of contacts remain the same from day to day.

——enthusiastic about having him
——pleased to have him
——satisfied to have him
——accept him with reservations
——reluctant to have him
——would not want him

Comments: ______________________

____

Assignment 3

One requiring the ability to deal effectively with people where he has the responsibility for their supervision.

——enthusiastic about having him
——pleased to have him
——satisfied to have him
——accept him with reservations
——reluctant to have him
——would not want him

Comments: ______________________

____

Assignment 4

One where contacts with others are in a staff capacity. Contacts vary from day to day and are made for such purposes as obtaining information, etc.

——enthusiastic about having him
——pleased to have him
——satisfied to have him
——accept him with reservations
——reluctant to have him
——would not want him

Comments: ______________________

____

(*c*) *A Branch Office Training Program.*—Another very large company has made use of a "loop" administrative training program since 1920. This program was developed to provide a satisfactory transition between the classroom and life insurance work for new college graduates. A senior officer of the company recalls that when it tried to put college men directly into group, claims, or underwriting work, two difficulties were encountered: the men were not sufficiently mature, and they were not able to grasp the whole picture of company operations. As a result, only a small number remained with the company very long. This company inaugurated then, and still uses, a decentralized training system in which each trainee is offered a year's study in a branch office.

The cashier, who is in charge of the administration of the branch office, acts as training supervisor for the trainees put in his care. The office supervisors and clerical personnel act as their instructors. The program represents a combination of on-the-job training and "book learning," and is divided into 14 phases. Each phase involves some area of branch office procedure, and is supplemented by a study of such topics as insurance fundamentals, history of the company, the contracts issued by the company, and home office operations.

For each phase the trainee studies appropriate printed material; then observes the activities at the desk where that phase of the operation is conducted; and, finally, takes over the desk himself with the clerk in charge sitting at his side. After he has mastered each phase, the trainee must take an examination which is sent back to the home office for grading. Along with each test, the company's director of training receives a confidential progress report prepared by the branch office cashier. Two examination failures are grounds for dismissal, but few failures are encountered among trainees who seriously apply themselves to the program.

Little correlation has been found between test scores and eventual progress with the company. This may be due to the necessarily wide variation in the teaching ability of the branch office employees. Furthermore, some may consciously or unconsciously coach the trainee to do well on the examinations, and others may not.

In addition to the training activities mentioned so far, each trainee must prepare answers to 100 correspondence problems and submit them to the home office for correction. These problems are typical of those a service office faces, and require that the trainee do a considerable amount of research to arrive at a solution. This activity also provides practice in business correspondence, since the solution to each problem is given in the form of a letter to a policyholder and is criticized in terms of tact and English mechanics, as well as for content. A self-study course in correspondence accompanies the project.

A branch office training program is held to have an important advantage over home office training programs in that it allows the trainee to come into direct contact with policyholders and their problems, and also to work closely with the field force. He familiarizes himself with home office operations through study of printed material and correspondence. This system also allows more individual attention to be given each trainee than would be the case if the whole group—which, in 1952, consisted of 51 men—were put through training in the home office. Obvious disadvantages are the lack of uniformity in the training, due to scattering the trainees throughout many branch offices; and the "second-hand" knowledge of home office operations afforded by this procedure.

An additional disadvantage is that the program is generally referred to among placement officers and other outsiders as a "cashiers' training program." As the layman thinks of a "cashier" only as someone who sits behind a cash register, rather than as the administrative director of a life insurance company branch office, this training course fails to attract college students until they are informed of its nature as a general administrative training program.

As a matter of fact, graduates of the course have been placed in all branches of the company. Since the program has been in existence for a relatively long time, it is possible to point to several assistant vice-presidents among the former trainees. Graduates are at present in the actuarial, home office administrative, underwriting, accounting, accident and health, legal, personnel, residential mortgage loan, and other home office areas, as well as in the field. Four agency managers are graduates of the program, although it is not intended to train salesmen.

The training director in the cashier's department is responsible for placement, and reports that it is difficult to keep his graduates in any of the lower positions for more than a year, because they are continually promoted to more advanced jobs. He notes a tendency to fill with first- or second-year trainees positions which formerly were occupied by experienced employees without college background.

Like most formal training programs, this one is expensive. It is estimated that $5,000 per year per man is expended. This includes the trainee's salary and the cost of home office and branch office supervision. It is particularly expensive because no production requirements are made of the trainee during the year program.

(*d*) *Duration of Training.*—In the last year or two, several companies have instituted administrative training programs for college graduates. These are also "loop" programs, involving on-the-job training in many departments of the company in accordance with a pre-arranged schedule. They require a relatively long training period, ranging from eighteen months to three years, and generally include a small amount of special classroom work in addition to attendance at L.O.M.A. classes held for all interested employees of the company.

While newly instituted programs tend to be longer than those of earlier origin, some companies have curtailed or plan to curtail the length of their "loop" programs. An official of a company at present offering a year of "loop" training feels that six months' exposure is sufficient. He believes that too much of the trainee's time is taken up with the performance of routine procedures under the year program. On the other hand, he would not like to see it so curtailed that the trainee gets no experience in clerical routine. He feels that experience in such routine gives an appreciation of the rank-and-file employee's point of view that is invaluable in future administrative work and that cannot be obtained in any other way.

One of the pioneers in college training programs now has a "loop" program lasting only four weeks. Under the streamlined procedure, small groups of trainees spend from one to eight days in each department of the company according to a pre-determined schedule. In the course of each visit, officers and other employees discuss and demonstrate the operations of their department. The following is an abstract of the outline, developed by this company's claim department, covering a one-and-one-half day visit to the department by the trainee group:

Officer D. Introductory Talk
- Company's claim philosophy
- Claim department in relation to other departments
- Agent's responsibility in claim work
- War clauses and war losses

Officer C. Discussion of organization and administration of units and field office

Officer R. Group insurance

- Comparison of the claim philosophy between group and ordinary insurance
- Trends in legislation affecting group insurance claims
- Coordination between hospitals and group carriers

Accident and Health Insurance—Claim examiner

- Method of payment of claims
- Handling of questionable claims
- Liberalizations from contract language
- Bases for denial of claims

Death losses—Claim examiner

- Methods of payment
- Means of investigating claims
- Reinsurance death losses

Disability claims—Claim examiner

- Ordinary life and group life

Field problems—Claim examiner

- Administration of field office
- Public contact
- Installation of group case
- Field investigations
- Coordination between agency, claim office, and home office

Accounting division—Officer B.

A new accident claim is followed as it goes on its routing through the clerical operations necessary in establishing a claim file. Following this, trainees sit in on one of the examining units and briefly observe how the various claims are handled.

Review with question and answer period—Officer W.

Trainees are given the facts pertaining to a claim and in discussion a course of action to be followed will be decided.

Another company is considering reducing still further the length of its "loop" program, which at the present time consists of a few days in each department. Department heads have informed the personnel director, who is in charge of the college training program, that the "loop" program is a "terrible chore" at this time. Supervisory people are burdened too greatly with the press of day-to-day operations to be able to give as much time to the trainees as they require.

(*e*) *Criticism of Loop Training.*—Certain aspects of "loop" training have been subjected to criticism, and it is noteworthy that large industrial firms have been curtailing their "loop" programs in the last year or two and are offering instead on-the-job training within a department, with job rotation taking place within departmental boundaries. Life insurance companies, in fact, are among the last remaining advocates of the "loop" program.

A number of points of objection to the "loop" program are raised in an article on the training of property and casualty field men.[5] This discussion is relevant to life insurance training programs as well:

> Unfortunately, the "loop course" has several very serious disadvantages. One of the most obvious is in supervision. With any sizable number of men in rotation, careful supervision of the individual is very difficult and standardization of training techniques virtually impossible. Frequently, the trainee is looked upon as a nuisance in the department. Since his stay is but temporary there is little incentive to do a thorough training job. Often his presence is resented by the regular clerks in the department, who feel he is a "fair-haired boy" receiving special treatment denied them. Furthermore, the trainee is exposed to such business as happens to be going through the department at the time: it may be a very unbalanced exposure. Added to all this is the fact that what was learned in the first few departments visited can become pretty cold by the time the last unit is finished.

In addition, salary difficulties arise. It is hard to evaluate the contribution of the trainee for merit rating purposes because he is unlikely to be in the department long enough to be an efficient producer. The supervisor will seldom concern himself with getting raises for the trainee, since he is more concerned with the welfare of his permanent staff. Token raises, uniform for all trainees, may not provide satisfactory incentive.

Objection is found also to the program which combines a half-day's formal schooling with half-time on the job. Difficulty in integrating work experience with the subject matter taught in the classroom is often encountered. It is claimed, also, that the immature trainee may "wander" between his job and the classroom, seriously abusing his working hours.

5. H. Paul Abbott, "How to Train Fieldmen," *Rough Notes,* XCIII (Dec. 1950), 36.

(2) *Classroom Training*

At least one life insurance company offers a straight classroom training program. In this course, 12 students, preferably holders of master's degrees in industrial engineering or business administration, are given a year's training leading to a position in management consulting work within the company. The program was established because of a conviction that experts in management rather than technical experts are required for administrative positions. As the training director remarked, "Just because a man is a good claims appraiser he need not make a good manager of the claims department."

When the program was first established in 1946, trainees worked on routine matters in operating units in addition to their schooling. This was later abolished in favor of full-time classroom training because the on-the-job training was found to be extremely time-consuming and unpopular with the students, who felt they were asked to work on "trivia." The present program has on-the-job aspects only in that the trainees are required to go to the company's files to get case material for class discussion.

The formal training begins with a study of life insurance principles and practices in order to provide a background for the trainees, who are not expected to have previous experience or training in insurance. After a phase devoted to the company's place in the industry, the student is introduced to office machines and punched-card accounting systems so that he may appreciate the management problems arising from the mechanization of clerical functions. Some of the more technical topics considered include forms design and control; simplification of clerical tasks; measurement techniques and quality control, as applicable to clerical processes; work scheduling and control; applied cost control; and techniques of conducting management surveys. A considerable amount of time is devoted to developing skill in working with people through training in conference leadership methods, interviewing techniques, report presentation, public relations, and supervision. The case method of instruction is used throughout in order to encourage original thought on the part of the student rather than merely to indoctrinate him with prescribed facts and ideas.

The next phase of the program is entitled "creative development," and involves tackling the management problems of a hypothetical life insurance company. The trainee learns the techniques of making management audits by planning a course of action designed to obtain information from a division manager in order to prepare a report suggesting areas of improvement. Practice in interviewing procedures is given by members of the training staff, who play the role of division manager and who deliberately seek to give the trainee a "hard time" by taking advantage of any personal weakness that the trainee exhibits. The trainee is finally given practice in "selling" his report to the top management of the company, impersonated by the training staff. Each trainee is given a major project in connection with the hypothetical company. Such projects have included the establishment of a midwestern head office, the equalization of the time of policy delivery to agencies in all parts of the country, and the production of policies and records by a multilith process. For his project the trainee must analyze the facts of the present situation; work out forms, space requirements, and procedures which will accomplish the required results; determine the costs of the proposal; and compare them with existing costs.

After seven months of such academic training, the trainee is assigned to work in a division of the company devoted to management consulting. Here he assists senior men in the division in supervisory methods standardization, involving merit rating, job evaluation, clerical and supervisory training, job relations, work simplification, and the like. He also works in the Machine Methods Unit, analyzing machine methods and their applicability to present requirements, and aiding in the installation of new machine systems. He also gets experience in the Forms Unit, which studies the design and use of the thousands of forms employed by this large company. The final phase of his on-the-job training allows the trainee to assist in actual management audits (made at the request of operating units) which suggest areas of improvement in organization, personnel, and equipment utilized in performing line functions.

In addition to the company whose management training program has just been outlined, the principal advocates of the classroom type of training are two property and casualty companies. Rather than interspersing on-the-job training with several hours a week in the classroom, as is the practice of most life companies, these two companies provide several months of uninterrupted academic instruction. One large company is unique in that it maintains a staff of 16 full-time instructors who have been recruited from the academic profession rather than from within the insurance business. The director of training of this company, a former schoolman himself, maintains that it is easier to make an insurance expert out of an experienced teacher than to make a competent teacher out of an insurance expert. Several students undergoing training have supported this proposition in conversations with the writer. They find that supervisory personnel, when called upon to lecture on their department's activities, tend to overwhelm the student with a mass of procedural detail, rather than effectively to present essential principles.

Young college graduates may be impatient with too extensive classroom training. They are eager to get out of the classroom after 16 years in its confines, and to start work. Furthermore, unless the trainee can relate the information dispensed in the classroom to his own work experience, he may be insufficiently motivated to absorb the large amount of detailed subject matter presented. One property and casualty company assigns the new college graduate to a branch office for six months before his schooling in order to give him some prior work experience in insurance.

Classroom training constitutes a relatively minor part of most training programs in other lines of business and industry, if data gathered in a 1947 study of 142 companies still present an accurate picture. According to this information, only 5 per cent of the company programs involved classroom training for more than half the time, while 58 per cent of the programs called for little or no time spent in the classroom.[6]

4. PLACEMENT OFFICERS' IDEAS ON TRAINING

What do placement officers believe to be the requisites of a good training program?

About half the placement officers polled indicated that they were not sufficiently informed to answer this question. The majority who replied did not concern themselves with the mechanics of training but stressed certain general principles which make training programs in any type of industry attractive to college graduates.

Of those who commented upon training techniques, a few mentioned the desirability of classroom instruction. One placement man calls for "a good and complete orientation course in the classroom, followed by practical work in the various departments (doing, not just observing)." Another believes liberal arts graduates should be taught the philosophy,

6. Stephen Habbe, *College Graduates in Industry*, p. 18.

history, and theory of insurance in the course of six months of classes, either half-a-day or full-time, five days a week. Most of the others assume that the training will be on-the-job and suggest that the trainee be exposed to all phases of insurance work by a carefully supervised rotation program.

The placement officers are not unanimous as to the optimum length for such a program, although one year was mentioned more often than any other time. Several believe this period should be the maximum and caution against excessive length, while others feel that the program may last as long as two years. One officer stated flatly that it should cover "225 class and work hours."

Recognition of the training program by top management was cited by several placement officials as an important general requirement. As one director put it, "the program *must have* support of top officers as a true supply source for executive work." Another point frequently made is that the trainee must be given an "opportunity to do work of some significance during training." "Eliminate routine assignments," said one. "Give trainees responsible assignments worthy of their college training." "Adequate supervision" by competent and interested training officials is considered a "must."

Many of those replying emphasized the importance of setting up clearly-defined goals for the trainee to achieve at the end of his training. There should be "a definite and clearly announced plan for promotion, if the man makes good, so he'll know what to expect." In keeping with this, several respondents urged that special care be taken in the placement of trainees in their first permanent positions and that their progress be subject to follow-up. An officer suggested that at the end of the program there should be a "frank conference between trainee and supervisory staff to insure proper placement."

While one officer calls for "a careful schedule, with clearly established hurdles and goals, stressing professional status, not salary," a good number of the placement officials mentioned the necessity of an adequate salary. A placement director reported that one of his graduates now enrolled in a company training program complained that he has to live on hamburgers and hot dogs all week in order to be able to take his girl out on Saturday night.

5. EMPLOYEES' IDEAS ON TRAINING

The group of college-level employees interviewed includes individuals who have been exposed to the "loop," branch office, and classroom type of formal training program, as well as those who have had no formal training. On the whole, those who were given the formal training found it to be worthwhile, while many of those who did not get such training believe it would have been valuable.

Graduates of the "loop" course agree that its greatest practical benefit is to acquaint the trainee with personnel throughout the company, because in their permanent assignments these individuals often have occasion to consult or work with people in other departments. While those interviewed do not minimize the value of such a program in giving the new employee an overall picture of company operations, they fail to retain much of the detailed procedures as carried out in the different departments. In fact, the major criticism of the "loop" course is that too much emphasis is placed on these details by personnel of the departments visited. "Too much pink card—green card stuff," was one comment.

As might be expected, the instruction tends to be uneven from department to department, with some supervisors offering a well-organized orientation program while others either are too busy to be helpful to the trainees, or "know their stuff but can't get it across." It was noted that the loop course is generally run in the summer, when many of the top men are on vacation, leaving the training to their subordinates. The trainees are, however, more interested in meeting the department heads than in learning the details of various clerks' jobs. The trainees generally appreciate being given work to do in the departments they visit, whether on actual business or on "dummy" projects. But those who had undergone the longer "loop" training programs deplored having to spend eight weeks on a dull task that could be learned in two.

Graduates of the branch office program described above found this experience valuable, particularly if their present home office assignment involves work with the field organization. On the other hand, they feel the course is designed primarily to teach branch office operations, with home office contacts so limited that familiarity with home office functions is not obtained through the program. It was suggested that a shorter period in the branch office be supplemented with a program in the home office for those receiving assignments there.

At least half of the college-level people sampled were assigned to a specific job without a formal training period. Their reports on their training experience vary with the job, the nature of their supervisors, and their own temperament and capabilities. Some stated they were given excellent on-the-job training by their associates and supervisors, who were always available for consultation. A notable example is found in the newly organized group department of one company where the work is almost as new to most of the senior supervisors as it is to the youngest trainees. Continual discussion among all members of the department makes the learning process stimulating and enjoyable. On the other hand, some people found that those assigned to train them on the job could explain procedural details, but had no idea of underlying principles. One man reports that his "teachers" would answer his inquiries as to why a certain procedure is performed, with: "We've done it this way for 25 years."

Many of those interviewed declared that being "thrown into" a job on one's own, without previous training, is the best and most stimulating way to learn, although, according to one man, "it is sometimes a little nerve-racking." These people, it usually developed, were given the benefit of excellent coaching by their immediate superiors. Others complained that in the absence of a formal training program they were left to "flounder around" without specific instruction or orientation. They often were unable to understand the instruction given by their supervisors because of their unfamiliarity with insurance terminology.

Employees of departments whose functions are interrelated with those of several other departments are more likely to feel the lack of a company-wide training program than are employees of relatively isolated departments. Many of the latter employees, however, recognize that while they have become highly competent in the work of their particular section or division through on-the-job training alone, more diversified training would better equip them to move into another function should the opportunity arise, and would aid them in obtaining managerial positions.

6. GROUP SALES AND SERVICE TRAINING

Because many life insurance companies entered the group insurance field a relatively short time ago, and because this type of coverage has expanded tremendously in recent years, the group department is often the fastest-growing segment of the company. A substantial number of college graduates is absorbed in group administrative positions, which tend to be less routine than similar positions in ordinary life administration.

In addition, most of the companies engaged in an extensive group business maintain staffs of salaried group sales and service representatives who are based either in the home office or in branch offices. This type of work is particularly appealing to college graduates who wish to get out in the business world and work with management in all branches of industry. At the same time, the sales and service representative works on salary, often supplemented by an incentive bonus, and has the security which straight commission selling lacks. Because this study is principally concerned with non-selling home office employment, only a brief summary of group sales and service training is given.

Of the 65 companies contributing to this survey, 26 write group insurance. Just under half of these companies have instituted formal training programs for group sales and/or service representatives. These programs devote a greater proportion of training time to classroom instruction than the programs for strictly home office positions. This instruction is followed by on-the-job training in a branch office. There is considerable variation in the duration of the home office training given the candidate for group sales and service work prior to his going out into the field. A four-week program seems to be the shortest; several run for two to three months; and at least one company exposes the trainees to home office operations for one or two years before sending them into the field.

For example, one company gives a six-month course of lectures for trainees in group service. These lectures cover the nature of the group policies written by the company; underwriting requirements; and accounting and administrative procedures. Upon completion of the course, the trainee is assigned to a branch office to gain experience in servicing employers who are covered by that company's group policies. This service includes aid to the employer in enrolling employees and in establishing an accounting system for administration of the group plan. A continuing relationship with the employer is maintained to keep the plan functioning satisfactorily.

In most companies, the group sales and service functions are not kept separate to the same degree that they are in the company whose training plan was just indicated. It is typical for a trainee to be exposed to the servicing phase of group activity first, and, after he gains experience and maturity, to move into the sales field. For example, another company gives its insurance sales and service trainee a four-week course in the home office group department. He then is transferred to a branch office, where he calls upon existing policyholders under the guidance of more experienced representatives. Gradually he is exposed to sales activities until at the end of two years he will devote most of his time to sales work. A considerably more extensive home office training period is afforded to candidates for group pension sales work by this company. Six months to a year is spent in all divisions of the home office group pension department before transfer to a branch office.

7. TRAINING FOR COLLEGE WOMEN

To what extent do life insurance companies offer formal training programs for women?

While two-thirds of life insurance home office employees are women, men constitute about 98 per cent of the company officers. Among the reasons cited for this discrepancy is the lack of training afforded women that would equip them for high-level supervisory, technical, and administrative positions.[7] Companies hesitate to enroll recently graduated college women in long and expensive training programs because it is generally felt that few of them will be with the company long enough to repay the investment made in their training. On the other hand, the Korea-induced manpower shortage among male college graduates caused many business and industrial firms to show increasing interest in the recruiting and training of women for jobs ordinarily held by men. A study of 36 firms in all branches of industry reveals that women are being recruited as chemists, accountants, engineers, statisticians, draftsmen, buyers, time study technicians, advertising assistants, production control people, and editors of house publications. Two insurance companies among the 36 firms reported recruiting female claims adjusters and underwriters.[8]

Some of the life insurance companies which maintain formal training programs primarily designed for male college graduates admit women to them as well. Of the 23 companies reporting a formal non-

7. See George E. Johnson, "Our Women Supervisors and Technicians," *Proceedings of the 1950 Annual and Special Conferences, Life Office Management Association* (New York: L.O.M.A., 1951), pp. 33-47.

8. Frank S. Endicott, "Trends in the Employment of College and University Graduates in Business and Industry" (Northwestern University, 1951), p. 8.

actuarial training program, 7 indicated that women are occasionally included. Generally speaking, however, these trainees are not new college graduates, but are women who have been with the company several years, who have made outstanding records in a clerical or supervisory capacity, and who intend to make a career with the company. Training directors are unanimous in reporting that such women hold their own in the classes and fully repay the company for training received by their job performance after graduation.

Although several companies actively recruit new female college graduates, they generally offer them positions for which relatively little training is required. At least two, however, have embarked on more or less extensive formal programs for new college graduates.

The actuarial department of one large company started its program in 1951, hiring 19 female mathematics majors from colleges in the vicinity of the home office. By the summer of 1952, 15 were still with the company; 2 left who did not care for the work; 1 married; and 1 went into teaching. It is the goal of the program to train the girls for moderately high-level technical positions within the actuarial department. The training involves placing the girls for two or three months in each section of the department until they learn the work. An assistant actuary is in charge of the program. He is responsible for recruiting the girls and for supervising them once they have been hired.

The company is highly pleased with the performance of the college girls. They are more mature and require less supervision than high school graduates who would otherwise have been hired for the positions. High school graduates of sufficient capacity to handle the complex work required in many positions in the actuarial department are increasingly difficult to obtain. The production of the group of trainees has been subjected to careful study, which revealed that the college girls match at least the quantity of output of non-college experienced employees doing the same kind of work. The quality of their work is not quite so good as that turned out by the latter group, since the college girls do not remain in a particular position more than three or four months.

The departmental officers indicated that they would be happy to have any of the girls attempt the Society of Actuaries examinations and pursue a full-fledged actuarial career. Six of the first group of trainees have expressed an interest in taking the examinations, and a few of these actually have taken one or more of them.

Conversations with a substantial number of the women revealed that they are quite happy with the program, although a few find the work somewhat tedious. They are uniformly glad that they are assigned to a given position for only a few months at a time; otherwise, they feel, the repetitive nature of the tasks would bore them. They reported that their fellow workers are helpful and friendly. Only one noticed some resentment on the part of the non-college help because the college women were rotated throughout the department and were being paid a higher salary for the same kind of work.

Another large company, doing a multi-line business, instituted a program three years ago for using college women in non-routine jobs. Under this program the company is willing to hire women who plan to be with the company at least one year. Training programs varying in length from three months to two years have been developed to fit the women for positions of different degrees of complexity. College women are recruited for work in three functions of the company: casualty underwriting, group underwriting, and actuarial work. Ten girls, on the average, are hired each year for each of the three divisions.

A six- to nine-month training process has been established for casualty underwriting. The college girl spends from two to six weeks in a rating unit, applying manual rates; she then moves on to work in a statistical unit, and in the accounting and other sections of the department, before being assigned as an assistant underwriter.

In the group department, girls are taken into the underwriting, statistical, contract, and accounting sections. In addition to attending a series of lectures on the social and economic aspects of group insurance, the various forms of group insurance policies, and underwriting and accounting procedures, the girls are given on-the-job training in the work of these sections. Members of the group underwriting department spend a considerable time servicing accounts in the field. Although no women have gone into the field as yet, some may enter it in the future. In the group accounting section, 400 high school graduate employees are engaged in billing and accounting work. College women are trained for supervisory positions which previously have been held by men.

College women who plan to be with the company for only a year are given two to three months' training in the statistical section of the actuarial department and are assigned to work preparing reports for rating bureaus and other associations from masses of statistical data.

Those who plan to stay with the company for a longer time are put into analysis work, in which they make studies comparing company with industry experience. They are also assigned to the group annuity unit and to special research projects. The exceptional girl may be prepared for liaison work between the actuarial and other departments in the company. This involves great technical competence in actuarial work combined with an ability to make explanations in language that can be understood by people outside the department. At present one college woman who has been with the company five years is performing this assignment.

The college women brought into the company under this program are under the general supervision of an associate actuary who is also responsible for their salary administration. He arranges conferences with the girls and with their supervisors every three months. Under the merit rating program, the girls are given formal rating by their immediate supervisors and by their division heads.

8. SUMMER PROGRAMS

Several companies have introduced summer training programs for college students in order to acquaint them before graduation with employment opportunities available in the home office and to be able to observe them at work prior to selection for permanent employment.

Actuarial departments have been active in organizing this summer work, generally for male juniors who have majored in mathematics. One company offers a 10-week training program each summer for six to eight female mathematics majors. These girls are given three weeks of orientation lectures, followed by instruction in probability and life insurance mathematics for part of the day. During the rest of the day, the students are assigned to work with members of the permanent staff for on-the-job training.

9. INTERNSHIP PROGRAMS

In early 1953, a large company announced the establishment of an internship program in its controller's department. Accounting majors from colleges of business administration are selected for several months' work with the company during part of their senior year. During this period, the students become acquainted with internal auditing procedures within a large organization. This internship program is similar to those established by several large public-accounting firms. These are reported to be highly successful by the accountants, placement officers, and students who have participated in them.

10. HUMAN RELATIONS PROBLEMS

What human relations problems are raised by the establishment of a formal training program?

Executives of companies which have not embarked on formal training programs for college graduates have indicated that, while such programs might be valuable in developing future officer replacements, the personnel problems they would raise would be so difficult as to make the programs unattractive. On the other hand, executives of companies in which such training has been established over a period of years are not at all troubled by the problems created. Although some friction between trainee and non-trainee may have arisen in the first years of a formal program's operation, it soon is taken for granted by the employees, and no major problems persist.

Problems involving actuarial trainees are probably less troublesome than those created by non-actuarial training programs for college graduates. While some officers report that the major problem in working with the actuarial trainee is keeping him satisfied while learning on the job, his path of progress is more clear-cut than that of the non-specialist, being based almost entirely on his own ability as revealed by success in the examinations. Most companies have established a formula whereby salary increases are awarded with the passing of each examination.

Because of frequent job rotation under most programs, the trainees seldom complain of too much clerical routine. As an actuary pointed out, a job is not routine until the trainee learns it. This may take him four months, and he is kept on the job only a few months after he has learned it before being shifted to another position.

One training officer reports that the trainees tend to become impatient with the methods prescribed for performing departmental operations. They continually suggest changes in procedures which would make, they believe, for greater efficiency. Frequently, however, the suggested methods are too complicated for the average employee to handle.

In the course of his training, it often happens that the actuarial candidate will perform the same job for higher pay than a regular non-college employee, but this situation generally causes little trouble. The non-college employee knows that the trainee must put in many hours in addition to the normal work-week in preparation for the examinations, and generally he does not resent the better promotion opportunities and higher salary scale granted to the trainee. One actuary noted that if other employees know the trainee is not competing with them for the next higher position there is little resentment, even though he may eventually be given a post several degrees ahead. Absence of friction is credited also to a careful selection process whereby candidates for actuarial training are judged on their ability to mix easily with the non-college employees as well as on their academic performance.

Officers in charge of actuarial training programs stress, nonetheless, the necessity of counseling with both the trainee and non-trainee to prevent any friction from arising. The trainees are cautioned against revealing to their fellow workers a feeling of superiority because of their better education. The non-college employees must be shown that the presence of the trainees will not close out their opportunities for advancement. There is the possibility, too, that non-college employees in supervisory positions may tend to show undue favoritism toward the trainees under their control because the latter may be their bosses some day. This attitude is discouraged for the sake of the other employees as well as for the trainees themselves.

More pressing human relations problems are likely to arise out of non-actuarial training programs for college graduates. Here the trainee is not necessarily set apart from the rank-and-file employee by his superior technical competence, but merely by his college education. In the course of a "loop" training program, as in actuarial training, for example, the trainee will often perform the same job as the non-trainee and be paid a higher salary. Some companies try to pay equivalent salaries for equivalent work, but most others pay more to college graduates for their "potential." The experienced employee will, more than likely, be far more competent at the particular assignment than the trainee, and may well be asked to help him learn the job. Since the trainee, furthermore, may be regarded as the "fair-haired boy," in line for promotion to the officer ranks, it is apparent that serious resentment may develop.

Training directors again emphasize the importance of trainee selection in minimizing this problem. The college graduate must have no delusions that his additional education automatically entitles him to privileges denied others. The graduate of one training program reports that, because his classmates were careful not to reveal a "fair-haired boy" attitude, they experienced no hostility toward themselves as individuals, although some company employees are resentful of the program as a whole.

Most companies have tackled this problem by allowing qualified non-college personnel to enter the college training program. Only one company was found which refuses admission to non-college employees on the grounds that it would not be fair to earlier trainees who have met the college requirement. Other officers indicated that because of the consequences for employee morale they would not dream of instituting a program limited to college graduates.

In actuality, a relatively small number of non-college employees have been admitted to these programs. One training director noted that if a regular employee possesses outstanding capacity, he will generally have advanced too far with the company to be willing to begin all over again as a trainee. If he has not advanced so far, he probably lacks the capacity to succeed in the program. On the other hand, 40 per cent of those going through one company's training program are not college graduates. The officer in charge reports that the college men generally do a better job, particularly in facing problems requiring analytical ability.

Another means used by several personnel directors to counteract resentment is to discuss the problem frankly with groups of supervisors. In these talks, it is pointed out that admission to the training program is no guaranty of promotion, although the odds are in favor of the capable trainee. The non-college employees are urged to avail themselves of the L.O.M.A. and C.L.U. courses in order to improve their own chances of promotion. Generally speaking, those companies which run formal college training programs also provide free L.O.M.A. classes. Employees are also encouraged to continue their higher education at night. Several officers have pointed out that unusually good executive material comes from employees who went to work immediately after graduation from high school but who obtained college degrees at night. Most of the companies, however, find they do not obtain today high school graduates with sufficient capacity and ambition to embark on such a program.

11. TURNOVER OF TRAINEES

Perhaps the personnel problem of greatest magnitude faced by the company which has instituted or which plans to institute a college training program is that of turnover. To the extent that a company retains its employees after it has invested considerable sums in training them, the program is successful. No matter how excellent the training given, if the graduates leave the company before it has realized its investment in their training, the program is often considered a failure, particularly by top management.

It will be recalled from Chapter One that 36 out of 45 companies found turnover of college-trained employees to be about the same as or lower than that of non-college-trained male employees. The 45 companies responding were divided into two groups—those which offer a formal home office training program and those which do not—in order to find whether the presence of such training tends to reduce or to increase turnover. The results are given in Table 29.

TABLE 29

COMPARISON OF TURNOVER AMONG COLLEGE GRADUATES WITH THAT AMONG NON-COLLEGE MALE EMPLOYEES IN LIFE INSURANCE COMPANIES MAINTAINING AND NOT MAINTAINING FORMAL COLLEGE TRAINING PROGRAMS

Turnover	Training Program	No Training Program	Total
Greater	4	5	9
About the same	4	12	16
Lower	6	14	20

Source: Questionnaires sent to life insurance company officers (see Appendix I).

From these figures it appears that in either case the turnover is about the same or lower for college-trained personnel. There does seem to be somewhat better experience on the part of the companies not offering training programs, but the sample is probably too small to make a meaningful generalization.

Most of the companies which are leaders in the field of college recruitment and training are quite pleased with their ability to retain college graduates after they have trained them. For example, one company reports that 20 out of its 28 trainees of the class of 1948 are still with the company; of the 1949 class, 17 out of the 28 remain; of the 1950 class, 13 out of 16 remain. Another company finds that it has retained more than 75 per cent of its college graduates. A third company made a study for the period from 1930 through 1950 and found an average termination rate of 12 per cent in the first year, 12 per cent in the second year, and then down to 2 to 3 per cent a year. These figures include terminations for all reasons, including entry into military service when the employee does not return to the company upon release.

These figures appear in an especially favorable light when compared with the results of a recent general industry survey. Dr. Robert N. McMurry conducted a study of 1,767 trainees hired from college by 247 companies in all branches of business and found that there was a 42 per cent mortality rate in the first year of employment. Dr. McMurry concludes that the major cause of turnover is lack of maturity on the part of the failures. Immaturity was evidenced by the absence of self-reliance and perseverance; by inability to accept responsibility, to get along with people, and to wield authority without causing antagonism; and by failure to consider personal goals as coincident with those of the company.[9] If this diagnosis is accurate, careful selection becomes the primary consideration in reducing turnover.

Perhaps the most important reason for termination in the life insurance home office is that the employee feels he is not making rapid enough progress. One training director stated that second-rate material is likely to leave the company; first-rate men make rapid enough progress, so that they are satisfied to stay with his company. On the other hand, personnel people in other companies are frank to admit that their graduates often can get substantial increases in salary by leaving insurance for industrial concerns in the first few years after training. Where the training program is not wholeheartedly supported by top management as well as by line supervisors throughout the company, turnover of training program graduates is likely to be an important problem. In this case, there may be such difficulty in placing and promoting training program graduates that they become dissatisfied, and quit.

9. Cited by Franklin H. Beardsley, Jr., "The Relation and Integration of College Graduates to and into Business" (paper presented before Sixth Annual Louisiana Personnel Management Conference, Louisiana State University, Baton Rouge, Louisiana, April 20, 1950).

After Training

Highlights of Chapter 7

Companies with formal training programs are evenly divided as to the timing of placement decisions: one third make permanent job assignments before training begins; another third, during training; and the remainder, after the training period.

College trainees are placed in both line and staff positions in companies with firmly established recruiting programs. In other companies, college trainees are generally assigned to staff specialist positions.

Vigorous company growth and the minimization of seniority as a factor in promotion reduce problems arising from the placement of college trainees.

Few life insurance companies have established comprehensive management development programs, although most of them engage in activities which encourage the development of management talent.

Programs involving organization planning, officer appraisal, and the development of an inventory of potential officer replacements have been inaugurated by some companies.

Development activities most often pursued by life insurance companies include supervisory training courses, committee assignments, "assistant-to" and staff assignments. Job rotation is considered feasible at the supervisory and junior officer level, but not for senior officers.

❋ *Chapter Seven* ❋

AFTER TRAINING

SUCCESSFUL programs for college graduates extend beyond the recruitment, selection, and training activities surveyed thus far. After training the college-level employee, those companies with well-organized programs give careful consideration to his proper assignment as a productive member of the home office organization. But it is felt by personnel people that the responsibility of the company should go further, that it should institute a long-range program of management development which will prepare the college trainees as well as other employees of promise for top-level positions.

Companies which make definite plans for the development of management-level personnel are attractive to the highest type of college graduate, even though he is asked to put in many years of work in the lower echelons. If, on the other hand, he is made to feel that he will occupy a dead-end job, and is not given a clear-cut notion of possible channels of advancement, he is unlikely to pursue an insurance career.

Those companies which have given serious thought to the problem of maintaining a reservoir of management material to replace top-level personnel as they retire are most likely to be concerned with obtaining their share of top-notch college graduates.

This chapter is concerned with problems of placement and of management development. In connection with the former, the following are considered: (1) the timing of placement decisions, (2) the positions in which the trainees are placed, and (3) major human relations problems which arise from the placement of college graduates in the home office. Then the paths of advancement are examined which today's senior officers have taken to reach the top, generally without benefit of formal executive development programs. Such programs are still practically non-existent in the life insurance company home offices studied, but certain activities which encourage the development of executive talent do take place. The chapter deals with the activities most frequently encountered, including (1) organization planning, (2) executive appraisal, (3) personnel inventories, and such developmental activities as (4) management conferences, (5) job rotation, (6) "multiple management" plans, (7) staff assignments, (8) use of understudies, (9) observational tours, and (10) outside academic training.

1. PLACEMENT

a. *When Placement Is Decided*

Most college-level employees are hired to fill specific positions, and their training is received on the job. This is true of companies without formal training programs and even of many which have such programs. Relatively few employees undergo the "loop" or classroom training programs discussed in the preceding chapter, before being given a permanent job assignment. Where the training involves exposure to a variety of company operations, one might expect placement decisions to be made after the trainee has gained experience in the different departments and has discovered where his interests and aptitudes lie. But only one third of the companies with formal training programs decide on placement at the end of the training period. Another third of these companies determine permanent assignments during training; and the remaining third, before the training begins.

In one company which makes the placement decision after training, each trainee is asked to write a memorandum indicating his preference as to permanent assignment after he has completed a year's "loop" program. The training director indicates that about 95 per cent of the men analyze themselves very well in making these requests. Occasionally they will apply for a position which does not seem in keeping with their interests and aptitudes, if they hear rumors of unusual expansion in one department and feel their chances for rapid advancement are better there than in some type of work for which they are more qualified. Responsibility for placement is in the hands of a committee consisting of the personnel director, the assistant personnel director (in charge of employment and training), the personnel administration director (in charge of promotion and transfer), the methods division administrator (in charge of organization and staffing), and the personnel research director (in charge of testing).

Another leading company which used to decide on placement at the end of the program currently assigns trainees to permanent positions before they enter the "loop" program. This is largely to discourage proselyting the trainees during their stay in the various departments. Departmental supervisors had tended to vie with one another for the services of the outstanding trainees, thus complicating both the training and placement problems.

The personnel director of a smaller company feels that its size is such that it cannot afford to bring in trainees without specific assignment. It hires college men for assignment to such general areas as group sales and service, actuarial work, or underwriting. Assignments are intended to be flexible, with every opportunity given the employee to change positions as his interests and aptitudes indicate. An important weakness in practice is that it is like "pulling teeth" to transfer a good man away from one department and place him in another. To overcome this weakness, the company is considering extending to three years the time during which the trainees remain under the control of the training department. It is suggested that their salaries be paid out of a training budget during this time. In this way, closer supervision can be exercised over the new employees, and they can be more easily transferred from one position to another in keeping with their interests and aptitudes until they find the job for which they are best fitted.

b. *Positions Assigned*

Into what positions are graduates of training programs placed?

Where the college program is firmly established in the company, either because it has been in existence for a long time or because it enjoys wholehearted top-management support, graduates of the program are placed in all parts of the organization, in both line and staff functions. For example, the graduates of the one-year "loop" program described above have been placed in 15 different departments of the company. The following are typical of these positions:

Administrative assistant in ordinary policy division
Methods analyst
Assistant sales promotion specialist
Labor relations assistant

Assistant claim adviser
Administrative assistant, ordinary agency department
Planning staff in group department
Assistant manager in claims department of Southwest office
Junior administrative assistant in treasurer's department
Methods analyst for machine operations
Junior underwriter
Junior security assistant
Assistant cost analyst
Employment representative
Auditing examiner

Trainees tend to fill a greater number of staff than of line positions. The training director reports that staff positions seem to have more appeal than line positions, which may involve more clerical detail than the training program graduate wishes to undertake. But there is no pressure, from either line supervisors or top management, to restrict the trainees to staff work.

In some companies, most college trainees, as well as college graduates who are assigned to positions without a preliminary general training program, are assigned to staff positions almost exclusively. A senior executive of one company, for instance, feels that a revolution would be started if college trainees were to be put into line supervisory positions. It is safer, he believes, to place them in specialized positions to which the non-college employees do not aspire. Another executive keeps his company's bright young college men "under wraps" in research and development work until they have been with the organization for a number of years. Then they may be inserted into the line. One personnel director places his training program graduates in staff positions just above the first line supervisory level. After they have proved themselves, they may be placed in second-tier supervisory positions.

c. *Human Relations Problems*

How are graduates of training programs received by supervisory personnel?

If these officials have themselves come up through the route of the college training program, there is presumably no problem. But in most companies, section and division heads have attained their positions after many years of line work, without the benefit of a college education.

Might these supervisors feel considerable hostility toward the trainee who is apparently being given opportunities which were denied to them? From reports of personnel people and directors of training, the reception given the college trainee by the supervisor varies with the individual personalities involved. In many cases, the supervisors are quite enthusiastic. One training director, for instance, finds division managers "crying" for his trainees. In fact, the managers put pressure on him through their vice-presidents to obtain as many as possible. It was noticed, too, how the "rushing" of trainees by supervisory personnel was a problem in another company. In only a few cases have supervisors accepted the training program graduates with hesitation. Generally speaking, this survey has failed to disclose widespread hositility toward college trainees on the part of non-college supervisors.

There are two highly important conditioning factors which either magnify or reduce the problems involved in placing the college graduate: one involves the growth of the company; the other, the importance of seniority in company promotion policy.

Some company officials report that friction resulting from the placement of college trainees simply does not arise because the company is growing so fast and in so many directions that there are more vacancies than there are qualified individuals to fill them. No one need fear, therefore, that the trainee will displace him from his job. When the company's growth is slow, however, there may be only a limited number of choice vacancies to which a large number of individuals aspire. In this situation, the college trainees may appear to have the advantage over employees who have not had college educations, and who may evidence considerable resentment at the better chances of the others.

The more weight given to seniority in a company's promotion policy, the more friction is likely to be created by a college training program. Where it is the company's express policy to promote on the basis of ability without regard to seniority, no problem arises when a training program graduate with relatively brief service is placed in a position for which experienced employees are also being considered, if it can be demonstrated that the younger man is best fitted for the job. If seniority has traditionally played an important role in promotion policy, there is likely to be widespread resentment. In the latter situation there is a greater tendency to keep college people in specialized staff jobs rather than to move them into supervisory line positions.

2. REASSIGNMENT

Attention was called above to an important problem—the maintenance of sufficient flexibility in the employee's permanent assignment so that he will not be forever wedded to a given position, whether or not it is to his liking. One personnel director, it will be recalled, advocates keeping college-level employees under his immediate supervision for three years to accomplish this.

Personnel and training people in companies with well-established college training programs make a special effort to watch over their ex-trainees lest they get "lost" or "stuck in a rut." Usually they keep up-to-date records of the present position and performance of each of the training program graduates, and are consulted by line management when vacancies occur.

But as was stated at the outset, the optimum solution to the reassignment problem involves a broad program of management development designed to equip high-caliber personnel for taking on greater responsibility and to provide clear-cut goals toward which they may strive.

3. TRADITIONAL PATHS OF ADVANCEMENT

Formal management development activity is relatively new throughout industry. Since World War II, many of the most prominent industrial corporations have evolved rather elaborate plans for the "growing" of executives within the organization. The vigor and recentness of this activity can be judged by the fact that the American Management Association published a bibliography of 241 titles dealing with this subject, only 19 of which predated World War II.[1]

The management development activity that is undertaken by the life insurance industry is of such recent origin that it has not influenced the paths of advancement of today's senior officers. What are the traditional routes to high-level positions in the home office?

Most life company personnel officials stress the importance of a "promotion-from-within" policy. Said one executive, "Promotion from within is a religion with us." Another wrote:

> We have a policy—always—of filling our top management positions from within. Hence, every position of importance in our Company at present is

1. For an expanded version of this bibliography, see M. J. Dooher (ed.), *The Development of Executive Talent: A Handbook of Management Development Techniques and Case Studies* (New York: American Management Association, 1952), pp. 553-71.

filled by a person who "grew up" here. Eighty-five to 90 per cent are filled with men or women who have spent their entire business life with this Company. The balance had some previous association of varying length or degree and came to us in beginner or near-beginner positions.

A training officer in one company maintains a file on the careers of the senior officers in his organization. One started as an office boy, 2 as mail boys, 15 as clerks, 7 as attorneys, and 7 as agents. On the average, it has taken 14 years for an employee in this company to reach officer status. This average would be higher if it were not for the presence of specialists (particularly in the actuarial department), many of whom achieve officer status in their late thirties and early forties.

One personnel officer notes that the traditional pattern from mailroom to company president is likely to change in the future. He feels it will more likely be from football captain and president of the senior class to president of the company. This is in keeping with the widely held opinion that a majority of the young men with managerial capacity today will not go to work immediately after high school in clerical positions, but will seek a college career instead. Other changes will be in the direction of accelerating the rise of capable young employees to top management positions. The mailroom-to-president route takes so long that the senior officer reaches his post when he is within but a few years of retirement. A company official pointed out that one cannot expect vigorous management by men who are preoccupied with their blood pressure.

An examination of the careers of a large number of top executives reveals that they generally rise within a given area of specialization. It is not until they reach vice-presidential status that they are required to concern themselves with company-wide problems. An overwhelming majority of company presidents, for example, reached their position through actuarial, legal, or investment channels.

There are companies today in which this traditional pattern no longer holds. In one large organization, 10 out of the 12 top officers came with the company through its college recruiting program. On the other hand, the president started in the mailroom but was so outstanding as to reach the presidency in his early forties. Rather than rising in one channel of specialization, he obtained experience throughout the company as a whole, heading the accident, group, and agency departments before achieving the top position.

4. MANAGEMENT DEVELOPMENT

A management development program suitable for the life insurance home office was outlined before the Life Office Management Association in 1947. The program, which is typical of similar activities in other branches of industry, contains five elements:

1. Organization planning to determine the company's present and future executive needs.

2. Analyzing the requirements of each key position.

3. Appraising executives to identify those with the greatest promotion potential and to determine their training needs.

4. Inventorying the availability and ready status of potential replacements.

5. Planning development programs to meet company and individual needs.[2]

"Organization planning" includes a thorough survey of the existing lines of organization by means of questionnaires completed by every employee with supervisory responsibilities. Through these questionnaires, those conducting the survey can discover what each officer and supervisor believes the lines of responsibility and authority to be. Overlapping functions, failure to provide for essential functions, conflicts in lines of authority, and other shortcomings of the present organization can be discovered and the organization plan revised accordingly.

Such formal organization planning requires that each executive and supervisor set forth his duties and responsibilities in specific terms, and from these statements the qualifications required for each position can be determined. A program of appraisal of all levels of supervisory personnel can be related to the job specification so developed in order to provide an inventory of potential replacements for each position. Finally, a long-range, many-faceted development program should be instituted to prepare company employees not only to move up to the next position, but to acquire sufficiently broad background to assume top management positions when the need arises. This development program may involve job rotation, committee assignments, internship

2. Ewing W. Reilley, "More Effective Management through Executive Development," *Proceedings of the 1947 Annual Conference, Life Office Management Association* (New York: L.O.M.A., 1948), p. 13. It is noteworthy that the American Management Association's handbook on management development, *The Development of Executive Talent,* is organized along the lines indicated by Mr. Reilley.

programs, "multiple management" plans, observation tours, formal classes, conferences, understudy positions, and other devices involving on-the-job as well as off-the-job training.

Only one out of 21 life insurance companies visited during the summer of 1952 announced that it had established a formal management development program. This is not to say that other companies are not engaged in activities which aid in the development of executive caliber personnel. One officer at first declared that his company had no executive development program, but conversation revealed that most of the activities which constitute such a program were being pursued in his organization; at the end of the interview he said, "If these things add up to executive development, I guess we're doing it." Smaller companies would hardly be expected to evolve elaborate and formal programs. Much of what must be deliberately planned in a large organization takes place naturally in a smaller company.

a. *Organization Planning*

In order to determine the extent of management development programs in life companies throughout the country, the questionnaire to company officers inquired as to their participation in typical developmental activities. The companies were asked, first of all, if they have undertaken formal organization planning to determine their present and future executive needs. Of 65 companies polled, only 7 replied in the affirmative; 5 others indicated that such planning was being considered. One officer replied:

> Functional planning [is] carried on constantly with increasing needs of company personnel a primary objective for supervisory and executive levels. All planning is supported by budgetary control on a departmental basis with a forecast at least three years ahead.

Another company engaging in such planning concentrates "in the area of plotting retirements which will occur in the next ten years."

While it might be contended that smaller companies need not be so concerned as larger companies with the formalization of organization planning, a top executive of a small company reports that it is typical of small companies not to plan far enough ahead. Personnel gaps are always springing open which must be filled on an emergency basis. He noted that the Life Office Management Association has recently set up a Company Organization Committee to help small companies with their organization planning.

b. *Officer Appraisal*

The questionnaire next asked if the companies had undertaken "a formal program of appraising junior executives to identify those with greatest promotion potential and to determine their training needs." Of the 60 replying, only 6 reported activity in this field, while 2 more are contemplating this move. One officer whose company has engaged in this warns that, while an appraisal program has been feasible for junior officers, senior executives are rather "touchy" about it.

Such appraisal extending to high-level officers is part of many management development programs in industry. For example, one manufacturing company has prepared an appraisal form for its supervisory and management personnel in which they are rated by three immediate superiors as to:

- Results
  - Quantity of work
  - Quality of work
  - Control of operating costs
- Methods
  - Planning and organizing
  - Getting along with others
  - Delegating responsibilities
  - Development of personnel
- Personal Adaptability
  - Knowledge of job
  - Leadership
  - Initiative
  - Dependability
  - Analytical ability and vision

For each category the appraisers are asked to give specific examples of outstanding results, successful methods, and strong personal qualifications; and also of poor results, poor methods, and personal weaknesses. The appraisers must indicate whether they feel the individual is well suited to his present work, and they must also recommend a course of action to improve his performance. The appraisal is discussed with the individual by his department head; he is asked to reveal what he himself believes to be his outstanding abilities, his ambition within the company, and what he is doing to improve himself, as well as his reaction to the appraisal. Finally, a confidential "evaluation of potential" report is prepared in which the next position for which he is qualified is stated, along with recommendations for additional experience and training which the individual requires to improve his promotion potential.[3]

c. *Personnel Inventories*

Many industrial companies have developed personnel inventory systems whereby the availability and ready status of potential replacements can be established. In a small company, an elaborate system is obviously unnecessary, because the senior officers keep such an inventory in their heads. In larger organizations, a more systematic inventory may be required. For example, one industrial firm prepares for its plants organization charts in which each supervisory position and its incumbent are shown. Each individual is further designated by two symbols, one indicating promotability and the other present performance. Different degrees of promotability include: "outstanding candidate," "average-to-good candidate," "questionable candidate," and "not promotable." Present performance ratings run from "not up to standard," through "doubtful because new," "doubtful," "good," to "outstanding." [4] Of the life insurance companies polled, 12 report they maintain some personnel inventory system, while four more are planning this activity for the future.

d. *Development Programs*

What progress have the life insurance companies made with respect to "development programs to meet company and individual needs"?

(1) *Supervisory Training*

A substantial number of companies have instituted a series of lectures or conferences for lower-level supervisory personnel. Of the companies polled, about one-third reported activity along these lines. Several mentioned company instruction and encouragement in the preparation for L.O.M.A. Institute Examinations as contributing to supervisory development. Some ten companies have adapted the wartime Training Within Industry courses for their supervisory employees. These consist of con-

3. See L. A. Russ, "Case 9: Westinghouse Electric Corporation," *The Development of Executive Talent*, pp. 419-45.

4. See *The Development of Executive Talent*, p. 549.

ferences to develop skill in leading (Job Relations Training), skill in planning (Job Methods Training), and skill in instructing (Job Instruction Training).[5] A distinctive feature of these programs is the use made of vestpocket-sized cards containing essential procedures and principles, rather than textbooks. For example, the Job Instruction Training (JIT) card contains the following:

JOB INSTRUCTION

How to Get Ready to Instruct (front)

Have a Time Table—

how much skill you expect him to have, by what date.

Break Down the Job—

list important steps.
pick out the key points.

Have Everything Ready—

the right equipment, materials, and supplies.

Have the Workplace Properly Arranged—

just as the worker will be expected to keep it.

How to Instruct (back)

1. PREPARE THE WORKER

Put him at ease.
State the job and find out what he already knows about it.
Get him interested in learning job.
Place in correct position.

2. PRESENT THE OPERATION

Tell, show, and illustrate one IMPORTANT STEP at a time.
Stress each KEY POINT.
Instruct clearly, completely, and patiently, but no more than he can master.

5. Developed by War Manpower Commission, Bureau of Training, Training Within Industry Service.

3. TRY OUT PERFORMANCE

Have him do the job—correct errors.
Have him explain each KEY POINT to you as he does the job again.
Make sure he understands.
Continue until YOU know HE knows.

4. FOLLOW UP

Put him on his own. Designate to whom he goes for help.
Check frequently. Encourage questions.
Taper off extra coaching and close follow-up.

If Worker Hasn't Learned, the Instructor Hasn't Taught

Case materials are often used to illustrate the principles and procedures outlined on the cards.

Some companies have developed their own programs for the middle management area. These programs may include the TWI courses or their equivalent, and then continue at a somewhat more sophisticated level. Many of the smaller companies have bought programs from management consulting firms, while the larger organizations have generally developed such activities on their own. One large company has embarked on a middle management development program to be presented in weekly two-hour lectures. An outline of the program follows:

A. *Organization and Planning*

Company organization and operation	6 lectures
Organization analysis	3 "
Procedures analysis	1 "
Work simplification	1 "

B. *Scheduling and control*

Establishing work measurement	2 "
Using work measurement	2 "
Scheduling flow of work	2 "
Controlling quality	2 "

C. *Mechanical and physical factors*

Mechanization of procedures	1 "
Forms administration	1 "
Space utilization	1 "

D. *Expense Control*

Budget preparation	1	"
Expense analysis	1	"

E. *Leadership*

Administrative practice	1	"
Administrative training	1	"
Selling ideas	1	"

F. *Public and Policyholder factors*

Supervision of correspondence	2	"
Public relations principles and practices	1	"

The training director who developed this program feels that supervisors in his company have an "overabundance of job competence" but need to know more about their company as a whole. He is particularly interested, also, in stimulating their "creative imagination."

(2) *Executive Seminar*

At least one large company conducts an academically oriented program on the top management level. Under the guidance of a professor of business administration of a leading university, a seminar in human relations in business is conducted for senior officers of the company. Cases taken from Glover and Hower's *The Administrator* [6] are used as the basis of discussion. The object of the course is to allow the officers to develop "administrative" attitudes by projecting themselves into the situations portrayed by the cases. An excerpt from the text's introduction defines the authors' concept of "administration":

> The qualities which, to our way of thinking, distinguish the administrator are his ability to think and act *responsibly,* to work co-operatively with others, and to provide others opportunities to work effectively and with satisfaction within the group.[7]

An officer of this company reports that its top executives have taken to the course enthusiastically and have benefited from it.

6. J. D. Glover and R. M. Hower, *The Administrator: Cases on Human Relations in Business* (Chicago: Irwin, 1952).

7. *Ibid,* p. 3.

(3) *Job Rotation*

Other significant aspects of management development go on outside the classroom. A device which has met with considerable favor in many branches of industry is that of job rotation between departments as well as within the department. Such rotation gets to the heart of one of the basic problems confronting life insurance companies: the lack of overall perspective on the part of employees who have specialized in one phase of the company's operations during their entire career.

Many prominent firms in other lines of industry have made rather daring experiments with inter-department job rotation on the very highest as well as on lower levels of responsibility. A leading public utility company has put some 220 officers through an extensive job rotation program over a ten-year period. Graduates of the program include the controller, assistant to the president, assistant vice-president, 13 department heads, 12 assistant department heads, 29 bureau heads, 43 general superintendents, 59 engineers, and 51 other professionals. To cite a typical case history:

Mr. A.—Background: Electrical Engineering. Length of service at time of appointment to program, 16 years. Position at time of appointment, Division Engineer, Electrical Engineering Department. His assignments were as follows: One year, Assistant General Superintendent, Underground Bureau, Outside Plant Construction Department. One year, Assistant Engineer, Electric Production Department. Third year, General Sales Manager, subsidiary company. Fourth year, Engineer, Distribution Division, Service Department of same subsidiary. Fifth year, returned to Company as Assistant Outside Plant Engineer, Outside Plant Bureau, Electrical Engineering Department. This completed his tour of assignments under the program. Since then he has been promoted to the position of Outside Plant Engineer, Outside Plant Bureau, Electrical Department, and more recently has become Planning Engineer, the Planning Bureau, System Engineering Department.[8]

In commenting on the job-rotation phase of the company's Executive Development Program, the personnel director writes:

If the E.D.P. [Executive Development Program] has done nothing else, it has over the years, as an inescapable result of moving key people around, broken down all those jealous and selfish walls that existed between companies, between vice presidents, and literally between departments...I don't

8. Dwight S. Sargent, "A Ten-Year Evaluation of a Job Rotation Program," *The Development of Executive Talent*, p. 265.

think anyone could ask for a more cooperative, considerate, understanding attitude toward what's best for the company than we have today. I can't set a price on it, but it's worth a lot.[9]

While a certain amount of interfunctional job rotation does go on in the life insurance companies studied, in none of those visited had a formal program of rotation been instituted with the primary purpose of developing executives. Of the total sample of 65 companies polled, 13 reported some interdepartmental job rotation. A wide variety of opinions was expressed as to the feasibility and value of such a program. One training director decries the lack of transfer across organization lines in his company, and would like to institute a formalized program similar to that described above. "We must," he said, "break down the path from the man under the supervisor to the supervisor so as to eliminate the attitude of many employees that if they keep their nose clean and sit long enough they will be the boss some day."

Several other officials, though fully realizing the benefits of job rotation, are aware of the possibility of disrupting the organization while carrying out the rotation. Where a full-fledged rotation program has not been established, practical difficulties beset sporadic attempts to transfer employees from department to department. Supervisors tend to keep good men to build up their own departments, and it is generally suspected that when initiative for the transfer comes from the supervisor, the employee is probably not very competent; he is not then welcomed by another supervisor.

A questionnaire respondent commented on the attitude toward job rotation prevailing in his company:

Our faults lie mostly in the job of training a man into a well-rounded manager or executive. The man who is good will get along to the top, but he may not have as good a picture of the whole as we would like. We are hoping we can correct this in the future by a more formal plan of job rotation.

The employment problem has been tough on the clerical level and therefore the young man who is capable is kept busy and hard at work at various learning jobs within his originally assigned area such as agency, accounting, investment, claims, etc., and the senior officer dislikes to let him go for trade with some other man because he is getting "work" out of the man—he is reluctant to start over again with a new man.

9. *Ibid*, p. 264.

We hope we can plan a program which will force rotation and schooling. Top management appreciates and accepts the need theoretically—but practically, is hesitant when it comes to their personal decisions involving their own departments.

No officer polled felt that interdepartmental job rotation is feasible on the senior officer level. On the other hand, rotation on lower levels is regarded more favorably. Ten out of 18 company officials responding to this question felt that this is feasible on the junior officer level, although it is not done extensively in most companies. One respondent wrote, "We do consider it feasible [on the junior officer level] and make effort to do it, but acceptance by top management is difficult." Sixteen out of the 18 respondents believe it is feasible on the supervisory level. This tendency to favor job rotation on the lower rather than the higher levels is at odds with the opinion held in some management circles that the higher the positions, the less technical skill and the more administrative ability is required of the incumbent.

More than half of the college-level employees interviewed expressed an interest in participating in a rotation program, but a substantial minority is less than enthusiastic. Some of the most recent employees wish to get established as specialists before they are subjected to rotation, while those who have a well-established position in a department, particularly if that department is growing rapidly, do not wish to jeopardize that position by transferring to other parts of the company. A junior officer in the agency department declared that the principles of management are the same, regardless of the department, and rotation would only acquaint him with details in which he is not interested anyway. Another individual criticizes a rotation program on the opposite grounds: one cannot learn enough in a short stay in a department to become a competent manager of that department. An older man who had been rotated from department to department in connection with his work in planning stated that he has become fed up with rotation and wishes to "settle down in one department and build something on his own." Others are afraid the program may be a waste of time unless it is definitely in preparation for management level opportunities.

(4) *Committee Assignments*

Interdepartmental committee assignments are often used as a tool of executive development. They allow members of the various departments to meet together to decide matters affecting the company as a whole. Most life insurance companies make more or less extensive use of such committees for the purpose of getting certain jobs accomplished. Their contribution to executive development is generally only an incidental by-product. Thirteen of the companies polled make use of rotating committee assignments for junior officers. At least one of these companies is consciously using such assignments to develop top management material. Some of the areas in which interdepartmental committees have been established include job evaluation, records destruction, manpower, lighting problems, pensions, salaries, suggestions, and interdepartmental coordination. A top executive of one company reported that his department heads are becoming much more "company-minded" and somewhat less "department-minded" as a result of committee assignments which allow for interdepartmental exchange of views.

(5) *Multiple Management*

Closely related to committee assignments, with perhaps more emphasis given to the developmental value of the activity, are various "multiple management" plans, which seven life insurance companies report they have established.

The pioneer in multiple management is McCormick and Company, the spice manufacturers, whose president in 1932 appointed 17 middle management men to a Junior Board of Directors with power to submit recommendations to the stockholder-elected Board of Directors. In 20 years, the Junior Board, along with a Factory Board composed of foremen and supervisors, has submitted more than 5,000 recommendations to the Senior Board, of which only 50 have not been accepted. Continued membership on the Junior Board depends on a rating by fellow members of the Board as to judgment, cooperation, initiative, poise, and human relations. The three lowest members are removed each six months, and the top six nominate the Board for the next six months.[10]

Seven life insurance companies indicated they have in effect some form of multiple management. Three have established junior boards of directors, presumably performing a function similar to the McCormick board. One company has a Junior Council, consisting of junior officers,

10. See Frederick J. Bell, "Highlights of Multiple Management," *The Development of Executive Talent,* pp. 109-14.

which makes recommendations to top management; another, a Middle Management Advisory Board.

(6) *"Assistant-to" and Staff Assignments*

A substantial number of life insurance companies, about one-third of those sampled, make use of "assistant-to" positions. Such positions have been utilized for training purposes where it is desirable for an individual to gain experience in a certain phase of work without assuming full responsibility. Assistants may be rotated from job to job without unduly disturbing operations.

Experts in executive development feel that staff assignments for line officers offer excellent training opportunities. These are described in one article thus:

> Staff assignments, perhaps more than any other, can develop an executive's ability to think clearly and handle people. The typical line executive spends most of his time dealing with routine matters. The staff man, on the other hand, has a minimum of routine and deals with new problems constantly, thus providing opportunities for improving his analytical ability through practice. Also, since he lacks line authority and must get results through persuasion, the good staff man acquires considerable skill in human relations.[11]

The large life insurance companies have a substantial number of staff positions which are available for development purposes. In Chapter Six it was indicated that graduates of college training programs are often placed in staff jobs for "seasoning" before assuming line positions. Companies maintaining a staff planning department, which advises the line organization on methods, systems, organization, forms, and procedures, find that this is a good training ground for future line officers.[12]

(7) *Other Devices*

There are other devices which make for executive development. Most operating officers, consciously or unconsciously, skillfully or unskillfully, train understudies. In many companies, an officer's own promotion is contingent upon his successfully training another to take his

11. Bernard J. Muller-Thym and M. E. Salveson, "The Tools of Management Development," *The Development of Executive Talent,* p. 73.

12. See George C. Boddiger, "Organization, Management and Control Activities of a Life Office Planning Division," *Proceedings of the 1951 Annual Conference, Life Office Management Association* (New York: L.O.M.A., 1952), p. 235.

place. Some companies make use of observational tours within their companies and in others to broaden their employees' knowledge. Life insurance companies seldom keep "trade secrets" from one another, and it is common practice to exchange information through visits to other home offices. Attendance at professional conferences is an important part of executive development in the life insurance business. Information is exchanged at meetings of the American Life Convention, the Life Insurance Agency Management Association, the Life Office Management Association, and other such groups.

A number of life insurance companies—generally the larger ones—have sent officers to management training courses given at universities. The Advanced Management Program at the Harvard Graduate School of Business Administration is perhaps the best known of these programs. Senior officers of several life companies have participated in this program, along with executives of other industries. A unique seminar in life insurance management problems was instituted for company executives at Columbia University in 1951. Representatives of different departments of leading companies in the New York City area have participated in discussions of company management problems, stressing the over-all aspects rather than specialized operations. One large company, for example, was represented by officers from the actuarial, the field management, the group, and city mortgage departments.

e. *Top Management Support*

Enthusiasm for the institution of management development programs was apparent among personnel and training officials of the companies visited. Such people keep abreast of the developments along these lines in other branches of industry and are generally eager for similar activity in their own companies. For example, the training department in one company has prepared a course in Management Training designed for top level personnel. The syllabus includes such topics as:

The benefits of management training—blueprinting future management needs—developing a replacement inventory—developing in the present job—using rotation of management assignments as a training aid—staff work as part of management development—the use of consultative management techniques—opportunities to use off-the-job training as supplementary program.

This program had not been sold, as of 1952, to the top management of the company.

Because technical specialists are found in the top positions of most life insurance companies, it is sometimes rather difficult for personnel people to convince top management of the necessity for a management development program. With conspicuous exceptions, few high-ranking life company officials are primarily experts in administration *per se*. As a result, some senior officers tend to regard management development programs as unnecessary frills.

But training officers interviewed stressed again and again the necessity of having complete top management support and participation in order to have a successful executive development program. If, for example, a program of supervisory conferences is instituted, top management must participate or middle management will tend to regard them as a waste of time. If a program of testing for appraisal purposes is put into effect, there will be considerable resentment on lower levels of supervision unless top management also submits to the testing. It is obvious, therefore, that the responsibility for a management development program must not be the training director's or the personnel officer's alone. Such officials, who have junior officer status in most companies, would certainly hesitate to appraise or to make replacement charts for their companies' senior officers. Responsibility for the program, it is agreed, must rest on a senior line officer, with the training or personnel department acting in an advisory capacity to aid in its implementation.

❊ *Summary and Recommendations* ❊

* Chapter Eight *

SUMMARY AND RECOMMENDATIONS

1. SUMMARY

SCOPE OF SURVEY

FIRMS in all branches of business and industry seek to attract top-flight college graduates to meet their technical and administrative manpower needs. This is a study of the role of the recent college graduate in the life insurance company home office. It is a survey of the attitude of the life insurance industry toward the college graduate, and that of the college graduate toward the industry. It is an examination of the nature of the employment opportunities available in the home office and the efforts of the life insurance industry to recruit, select, train, and develop its share of this important segment of the labor force.

SOURCES OF INFORMATION

Information for this study was provided during the summer and fall of 1952 by officers of 65 life insurance companies located in all parts of the country. While data were obtained from seventeen of the largest 20 companies, small and medium-sized organizations are well represented in the survey. Placement directors of 65 colleges and universities also contributed information, as did 65 recent college graduates who rejected positions with life insurance companies. In the summer of 1953, 68 college-level employees in nine home offices were interviewed.

a. THE LIFE INSURANCE COMPANY LOOKS AT THE COLLEGE GRADUATE

PROPORTION OF EMPLOYEES COLLEGE-TRAINED

In the typical life insurance company home office, a proportion of between 10 and 50 per cent of the male employees have a college education, but less than 5 per cent of the female employees have gone beyond high school. About three-fourths of the senior officers and more than half of the junior officers have received the benefits of a higher education. In recent years, an increasingly large proportion of new male employees have been recruited from the colleges. Some companies report that, except for building maintenance personnel, they have ceased hiring high-school-level males. But the majority of the companies polled still hire at least one high school graduate for every college man. The opinion is widely held by company officers that boys seeking home office employment directly from high school today are of lower caliber than those who joined the company from high school 20 years ago or more. The bright and ambitious high school boy, it is felt, will find a way of going to college.

POSITIONS FILLED BY COLLEGE GRADUATES

More life insurance companies hire new college graduates as actuarial trainees than in any other capacity. Other positions frequently mentioned are in the areas of accounting, underwriting, security analysis, claims, personnel work, mortgage analysis, statistics, methods, group policy-holder service, and advertising. Young college graduates generally prefer staff to line positions; the former are believed to be more glamorous than the latter, which are considered routine.

APPRAISAL OF COLLEGE GRADUATES

Some company executives are not anxious to hire an ever increasing number of college graduates. They believe that practical apprenticeship is more important than higher education and that the necessary academic training can be obtained in such courses as those preparing for Life Office Management Association Institute Examinations. They accuse college graduates of wanting to be vice-president within six months, or of being too preoccupied with vacations and fringe benefits. On the other hand, officers of those companies which hire large numbers of college graduates are generally pleased with the adequacy of their college training, their ability to get along with others, and their attitude toward job responsibilities.

Biggest Problem

The problem encountered most often in working with the young college graduate after he has been hired is his desire to progress more rapidly than the organization will allow, or more rapidly than his capabilities permit. This problem was mentioned to the exclusion of almost any other and is attributed to the natural restlessness of youth, impatience on the part of the veteran to make up for time lost in military service, and a desire on the part of the employee to achieve the living standards of his parents as rapidly as possible. In a majority of the companies, however, this restlessness does not result in higher turnover among college-trained than among non-college personnel.

Relations with Non-College Employees

Harmonious relations usually prevail between college and non-college employees, in the opinion of the majority of the officers and college-level employees polled. This is credited to proper selection and orientation. Somewhat more antagonism is noted on the part of older employees than among recent non-college employees. Officials of some companies which do not offer an organized training program for college graduates believe that non-college employee attitude is satisfactory at present, but that resentment would develop if such a program were instituted. Companies with considerable experience in such training find this fear unfounded.

FUTURE OFFICER REPLACEMENT: A DILEMMA

Officers of a majority of the companies polled feel that they are obtaining a sufficient number of college graduates to satisfy their immediate needs. This is true of those companies which are not convinced of the wisdom of employing large numbers of graduates and also of those with organized college programs which have managed to fill their annual quotas. In many instances, companies are meeting their present needs but cannot meet long-run requirements, specifically for the eventual replacement of junior and senior officers. An unfortunate dilemma confronts these organizations: on the one hand their officials feel that their companies cannot absorb more college-level employees at the moment, while on the other hand, they foresee difficulty in obtaining officer material in the future unless they bring in more college-trained personnel at the present.

b. THE COLLEGE GRADUATE LOOKS AT THE LIFE INSURANCE COMPANY

LIFE COMPANIES DO NOT OBTAIN "FAIR SHARE" OF COLLEGE GRADUATES

College and university placement officers agree four-to-one that the life insurance industry is not obtaining its "fair share" of top-notch college graduates. There are however, about four or five companies which are continually cited for their success in attracting first-rate talent. These companies are outstanding in that they employ a full-time college recruiting staff which generally operates out of the home office; they have a careful selection process which involves a visit to the home office at company expense; they have a formal training program; and they are concerned with the proper placement of the graduates after training.

Popularity of Life Insurance Career

According to the placement officers, insurance is considered one of the least glamorous industries by today's college graduate. Only a very small proportion of the typical graduating class has given any thought to an insurance career. Knowledge of non-sales opportunities in life insurance is almost universally lacking, and life insurance employment is considered synonymous with sales on commission.

Starting Salaries

The enthusiasm of those students who are informed as to home office opportunities is frequently dampened by the relatively low starting salaries offered by most life insurance companies. Placement officers generally agree that public accounting, industrial accounting, tangible sales, and production management positions commanded higher starting salaries in 1952 than did home office positions. On the other hand, starting salaries in banking, intangible sales, retailing, and utilities are considered about equal to those in life insurance.

Popularity of Fire and Casualty Companies

Most placement officers believe that property and casualty companies are more popular with their students than life companies, despite the fact that the latter are better known and the best life insurance company college programs are considered as good as or better than the best provided by the fire and casualty firms. The superior appeal of the property and casualty company is attributed to the average student's desire to avoid sales on commission, with which life insurance employment is identified. Life insurance companies, however, are not competing against other segments of the insurance industry for a well-defined group of college graduates especially trained for and dedicated to a career in insurance. They are competing with leading firms in all branches of industry for the top-notch college product.

WHY HOME OFFICE EMPLOYMENT IS REJECTED

The recent college graduates who were offered life insurance company positions, but who rejected them, were asked to indicate the critical factors influencing them to seek employment elsewhere. Low starting salary was mentioned most frequently, although a substantial number considered this relatively unimportant. Only one of the 31 males supplying this information took a position paying a lower starting salary than was offered him by the insurance company. A majority of the female respondents were also disappointed in the starting salary, but 7 of them went to work elsewhere for less money. A majority of the men also believe that opportunities for salary advancement are inadequate in insurance. Few of the women considered this, since, with notable exceptions, they do not look forward to a lifetime business career. Poor opportunities for advancement in responsibility, closely related to salary advancement, were also cited.

More than half of the respondents found fault with the nature of the work they would be called upon to perform in the life insurance company home office. "Dull" and "routine" are the most frequently applied epithets. More women rejected employment on this ground than on any other.

WHY HOME OFFICE EMPLOYMENT IS ACCEPTED

Few of the college-level home office employees interviewed had decided upon an insurance career while undergraduates. Nearly one-quarter had been interviewed on campus and convinced of opportunities by a company recruiter, while a substantial number became interested in insurance because of family connections. More than half seem to have stumbled upon insurance employment by chance.

c. AN APPRAISAL OF HOME OFFICE EMPLOYMENT OPPORTUNITIES

ADVANTAGES AND DISADVANTAGES

The advantages of home office employment most often cited by company officers are: opportunity for advancement, security, good working conditions, excellent growth record of the company, fringe benefits, good salaries, training program, and favorable location. Low pay and, paradoxically, slow advancement were mentioned as the principal disadvantages.

The appraisal of home office employment by the college-graduate employees interviewed is not dissimilar to that of the officers. "Good prospects for advancement" was most often mentioned as the reason why the individual had stayed with the company. "Nature of the work" took second place, followed by good working conditions, security, and adequate salary. Low pay compared with industrial employment, and poor location, particularly in the case of New York City companies, were the most often-cited disadvantages.

ADVANCEMENT OPPORTUNITIES

None of the employees indicated that slow advancement is an important shortcoming of home office employment. In fact, of the 68 employees interviewed, only 7 feel their prospects for advancement are poor. They are optimistic if those ahead of them are near retirement, if the company encourages lateral transfers across divisional and departmental lines, if the company sincerely adheres to a policy of promotion from within, and if seniority is not stressed in promotion decisions. Opinion is divided as to whether advancement opportunities are better in the larger or the smaller companies.

SECURITY

There is probably no commercial employment which offers greater stability and security than a life insurance company home office position. Wholesale dismissals of employees in times of depression are unknown, and some companies actually added to their staffs during the last depression to service the increased volume of policy loans. This job security is considered very important by less than half the college-level employees interviewed. Nearly a third declared that it is of no importance to them at all.

WORKING CONDITIONS

Working conditions are considered ideal in most home offices, which typically provide a shorter work week and more holidays than other white collar employment. More important to the employees polled, however, are the pleasant working relationships and the friendly, relaxed atmosphere obtaining in most home offices. Extremely large companies, however, have occasionally been criticized for regimenting their employees to an oppressive extent.

FRINGE BENEFITS

Substantial fringe benefits characterize many life insurance company employee programs. Two companies estimate that they provide employee benefits worth $1,500 per year. On the other hand, industrial firms have added so much in fringe benefits in recent years that the life insurance home office is losing its relative advantage on this account.

SALARIES

Starting Salaries

In 1952, life insurance companies of all sizes located throughout the nation offered an average starting salary of $225 to $250 per month to inexperienced college graduates without special training. The highest starting salaries reported were $300 per month, and the lowest $200. The largest companies tend to pay somewhat more than the smallest. Companies hiring actuarial trainees offer them a higher starting salary; $275 to $300 per month is the most frequently cited salary range for trainees who have not passed any Society of Actuaries examinations. The few companies which have had experience in hiring holders of master's degrees in business administration offer them about the same pay scale as actuarial trainees.

Five-Year Percentage Increase

The average 1952 salary earned by a college graduate who had entered the life insurance home office five years previously and who had made "average" progress with the company was between $375 and $400 per month. Of the 43 companies reporting, none paid such an individual less than $300 and 7 paid him more than $450 per month. This represents an average percentage increase over his 1947 starting salary of between 76 and 100 per cent. Comparable data have been published for graduates in all branches of industry and reveal an average five-year percentage increase of 76 per cent in engineering, 79 per cent in accounting, 97 per cent in sales, and 81 per cent for those who started in general administrative training programs. On the basis of these percentage increases, one must question the apparently widespread notion that salary advancement in the home offices of life insurance companies is considerably slower than in other fields.

Salary Satisfaction

Only 8 of the 68 college-level employees interviewed are definitely displeased with their present salary; 29 are pleased, while the remainder regard it as "so-so". More than half of this group is well-satisfied with prospects for salary advancement, a minority being barely satisfied or displeased.

Salary Structure in 50 Companies

Fifty life insurance companies provided information on the salary distribution for male technical and administrative employees with five or more years' service. Some 80 per cent of these home office employees made over $5,000, and 40 per cent were paid $7,500 or more in 1952. Nearly 3 per cent earned more than $25,000. Group sales and service personnel appear to receive lower salaries all along the line than the general run of home office employees, but these salaries are frequently augmented by bonus and commission arrangements. The agency management staff, on the other hand, tends to be better paid than the home office staff, particularly at the lower levels. In the higher brackets the salary scales of the two groups are similar. About 10 per cent of both drew salaries in excess of $15,000.

Large Companies *vs.* Small

Larger companies tend to pay better salaries than smaller ones, particularly to junior employees, and, of course, to those at the top executive levels. More than 40 per cent of male home office employees received less than $5,000 in 17 companies with assets under $100 million, while only about 16 per cent of comparable employees in 7 companies with assets over $1 billion made less than this amount. A comparison between a group of stock life insurance companies and a group of mutuals consisting of companies of comparable size revealed little difference in pay scales. A slight advantage was noted for the mutuals, but this is so small that one cannot conclude on this evidence alone that mutuals pay better salaries than stock companies.

Stock *vs.* Mutual

COMPANY GROWTH

A good company growth record is particularly important where many young college graduates are employed, since growth companies are better able to cope with their employees' eagerness to advance to new positions of responsibility. A company's recent entry into new lines of coverage opens more job opportunities for college people than mere increases in the amount of ordinary insurance in force. The introduction of group and accident and health coverages has necessitated the staffing of a wide variety of technical positions which absorb a large proportion of the college graduates in a home office.

NATURE OF WORK

Practically all the college-level employees interviewed, most of whom hold technical rather than supervisory or clerical positions, enjoy their work. Fifty-one of the 68 employees canvassed find their jobs a challenge to their full ability some or all of the time, although many acknowledge that a certain amount of routine detail work is inescapable; this, however, they do not consider overly oppressive. While most of those interviewed report they are under some pressure part or all of the time, home office operations are carried on at a relatively relaxed pace compared with "high pressure" types of employment. The increasing use of electronic computers in the performance of routine operations is raising the proportion of technical, as opposed to purely clerical, jobs available in the home office.

PRESTIGE

The prestige of life insurance home office employment is considered by a majority of the employees interviewed to be a neutral factor in attracting college graduates. Except for actuaries, home office employees are believed to enjoy less prestige than members of the learned professions or employees of the leading industrial firms, to rank evenly with those in banking and above those in retailing.

d. RECRUITING COLLEGE GRADUATES

College recruiting for home office positions came into its own during the post-war period, although 7 of the 65 companies polled actively recruited college graduates prior to 1930.

COMPANY RECRUITING PLANS

Twenty-six of the companies have no formal recruiting plan. A sufficient number of college graduates apply directly to meet the company's needs. Recruitment is decentralized in eight other companies, but a central office assists department heads and/or branch managers in their college contacts. Twenty-eight maintain a centralized recruitment office for college contacts. In six of these, a centralized office fills sales as well as home office positions. Variations of these basic patterns are found in the other companies.

Centralization

Placement officers in Southern and Eastern colleges overwhelmingly prefer centralized recruiting. They are greatly annoyed when several representatives of the same company contact them at various times during the year. While some placement people refuse to receive life insurance company branch managers and general agents, a majority of the placement directors polled feel that these individuals may successfully recruit for home office as well as for sales positions if they are well informed as to home office opportunities, and if they do not put undue pressure on the candidates to enter sales instead.

CAMPUS CONTACT

Most insurance companies queried do not maintain continuous contact with the placement office; only 19 reported that they visit one or more college placement offices each year. Most companies limit their recruiting to a few local colleges, although one large company attempts to cover 500 institutions throughout the country through its branch managers. Companies which have established full-time recruiting staffs usually visit 40 or 50 colleges a year. A few company recruiters make use of newspaper advertisements and employment agencies for college-trained personnel. Opinion is divided on their usefulness.

Placement Officer Attitude

Company personnel officers are favorably impressed, by and large, with the cooperation extended by the college placement officers. The latter are reported to be more cordial to home office recruiters than to representatives of branch offices or general agencies. The great majority of college placement officers believe the caliber of life insurance company recruiters is at least as high as, if not higher than, that of recruiters from other branches of industry. Most uncomplimentary remarks were directed toward recruiters for sales, rather than for home office, positions.

Recruiting Literature

Only seven of the companies polled publish literature specifically designed to attract college graduates to home office employment. Placement directors generally approve the brochures which are available, and are disappointed that more companies do not issue them, since they feel that recruiting literature is crucial in attracting students to an insurance career.

e. SELECTION

SELECTION CRITERIA

Personal Qualities

Those companies which hire substantial numbers of college-trained individuals have summed up the qualifications desired in this type of employee on the basis of job analyses. Creative ability, initiative, resourcefulness, and dependability, as well as intelligence, rank high among the qualifications specified.

College graduates employed in the home office rate "ability to get along with others" as the most important attribute of a happy and successful home office employee. In selecting new employees, they would also stress maturity and stability. Several suggested that married applicants are desirable in that they are more appreciative of the security offered than single people. Exceptional academic ability is not considered a prime requisite, except for actuarial trainees.

Educational Requirements

Life insurance recruiters, particularly those of larger companies, are willing to interview graduates who have pursued almost any course of study. A somewhat greater number of candidates is hired from schools of business administration than from liberal arts colleges, but many personnel officials, especially in New England, tend to favor graduates of the latter. While business administration students are preferred for accounting and investment positions, and mathematics majors for actuarial work, personnel people do not require specific educational background for other positions. College courses in life insurance or in general insurance taken prior to employment are seldom considered essential, although most officers think they are desirable. Smaller companies tend to consider previous study of insurance more valuable than larger organizations do, because it is too heavy a burden on the small company to train the "raw" college graduate from the beginning.

Actuarial Trainees

Many actuarial officers indicated a preference for individuals who majored in mathematics in liberal arts colleges, rather than for the products of universities offering special programs for actuarial candidates, because the latter graduates tend to specialize too narrowly in actuarial science. The officers seek well-rounded individuals who will make good administrators rather than mere technicians. Liberal arts mathematics majors are difficult to obtain, however, because the best ones are encouraged to enter graduate work; thus more companies recruit a larger number of actuarial trainees from universities with the specialized programs than from liberal arts colleges.

SCREENING PROCESSES

Elaborate screening processes have been established by those companies which hire large numbers of college graduates. In a typical procedure, a preliminary interview is held on the campus by the official in charge of recruitment, and successful applicants are invited to the home office at company expense for one or two days of testing and interviews with departmental officers and supervisors. Company officials estimate that it is necessary to interview anywhere from 16 to 138 graduates on the campus in order to hire one individual.

Aptitude Tests

Twenty-nine of the companies polled use aptitude tests in their selection process; 17 employ mental level tests; 11 use some kind of personality test; and 9, an interest test. Most frequently mentioned is the Life Office Management Association Examination in Clerical Work, which is generally used for all new "white collar" employees regardless of their educational background. Other tests frequently used include the Wonderlic Personnel Test, the Kuder Preference Record, the American Council on Education Test of Mental Abilities, and the Clark Activity Vector Analysis. Only a few companies have studied the validity of the screening tests they use.

Interviews

Personnel officials agree that the most important part of the selection process is the series of interviews. In companies where college recruiting is on a formal, continuing basis, interview rating forms have been developed. One company has issued an interview manual which suggests to the interviewer how to ascertain personality characteristics which are considered important to predetermine, but which may not be readily apparent.

f. TRAINING

TRAINING PROGRAMS A "MUST"

College graduates express a strong preference for companies which offer an organized training program. Convinced of the value of education, they feel that their chances of success in a particular field of business will be enhanced by thorough training. Training programs offer a sense of security to the new college graduate who may be afraid to plunge into the business world strictly on his own after a relatively sheltered and closely supervised educational experience. Also, the larger the investment a company makes in training a new employee, the less likely it is to discharge him after only a brief period of employment.

ORIENTATION PROGRAMS

Twenty-nine out of 47 companies providing this information carry on formal orientation programs for new employees. These run from 2½ to 12 hours, and typically cover the employee's benefits and responsibilities, a brief introduction to life insurance, the major functions of the company, and the way it is organized to carry them out. While orientation programs are valuable in making easier the induction of new college graduates into the home office, they are not what the college student contemplates when he expresses preference for companies offering formal training programs.

ACTUARIAL TRAINING

Formal actuarial training programs are maintained by 14 out of 48 companies responding. Several others indicated that although no formal program exists, actuarial trainees are rotated from job to job in order to get experience for the examinations. Formal training programs are similar in the different companies, since their common objective is to prepare the trainees for the Society of Actuaries examinations. A typical program involves 20 to 35 hours of study in addition to the regular work week. The trainee begins on routine clerical assignments within the actuarial department, and gradually progresses to positions which require greater technical competence and involve supervision over other employees. One hour per day of classroom instruction, either on company time or after the work day, is frequently provided. Because the actuarial examinations embrace so many areas outside of the actuarial department, experience in the operations of other departments is obtained, sometimes by actual work on the job, but more often by observation.

NON-ACTUARIAL TRAINING

It has been difficult to determine from its questionnaire response whether a company maintains a formal non-actuarial, administrative training program. Some companies merely encourage study for the L.O.M.A. examinations; and others confine their activities to on-the-job training, without providing special supervision for the college-level trainees. If formal home office training is defined to exclude such limited activities, 23 of the companies appeared to be conducting *bona fide* formal home office training programs. Most of these are relatively new; although some were in operation in the 1920's, the largest number have been inaugurated since 1946.

"LOOP" PROGRAMS

Those life insurance companies which have gained reputations for maintaining the best training programs make use of "loop" training, classroom training, or both. Under the "loop" program, the trainee spends a designated length of time in each of several departments of the company, actually working on-the-job in some cases and merely observing in others.

Small Company

An extremely small company currently has five trainees undergoing a comprehensive program in which they spend from two to eight weeks in each of fifteen departments. Early in the training, they are actually put in charge of the Office Services Department. After permanent assignment, each training program graduate must study for a Fellowship in the L.O.M.A. Institute and for the Chartered Life Underwriter designation, complete a home study course developed within the company, and sell at least $100,000 of insurance in order to familiarize himself with the problems of the field forces.

Large Company

A very large company has a college training program which is not fundamentally different from the one just outlined. Most of the college graduates hired each year are placed immediately in specific positions, but 12 with particular promise are given a one-year home office training program in which they spend time in underwriting, accounting, servicing business in force, claims, group insurance, methods, and in a district office.

Branch Office Program

Another very large company uses a decentralized training system in which each trainee spends a year studying the operations of a branch office. The program represents a combination of on-the-job training and "book learning," and is divided into 14 phases, each involving some area of branch office procedure, and each supplemented by a study of such topics as insurance fundamentals, history of the company, the contracts issued by the company, and home office operations. After he has mastered each phase, the trainee must take an examination, which is forwarded to the home office for grading, along with a confidential progress report prepared by the branch office cashier. In addition, each trainee prepares answers to 100 correspondence problems which are typical of those faced by a branch office.

Duration of "Loop" Course

Several companies have instituted, in the last year or two, administrative training programs ranging from 18 months to three years in duration. On the other hand, most companies with programs which have been in operation for many years have curtailed the length of their training period. One of the pioneers in college training now has a "loop" program lasting only four weeks. When the program was longer, the trainees found it difficult to retain much of the information dispensed in the many lectures and conferences scheduled. They noted that the principal benefit that they derived from the "loop" program was an acquaintance with personnel and with the positions available throughout the company, and they contend that this can be accomplished in a shorter period.

CLASSROOM TRAINING

At least one life insurance company offers a straight classroom training program. In this course, 12 students are given a year's training leading to a position in management consulting work within the company. Among the subjects studied are office machines and punched-card accounting systems, forms design and control, simplification of clerical tasks, and measurement techniques and quality control. A considerable amount of time is devoted to developing skill in working with people through study of conference leadership methods, interviewing techniques, report presentation, public relations, and supervision. The case method of instruction is used extensively in order to encourage original thought on the part of the student.

APPRAISAL OF TRAINING

By Placement Officers

Placement officers queried as to the requisites of an optimum training program declared that it must have the genuine support of top management; that the trainee must be given work of significance during his training; that clearly defined goals for the trainee must be set up; and that an adequate salary must be provided during training. Some advocate classroom training, but most of the others assume that training will be on-the-job and suggest that the trainee be exposed to all phases of insurance work in a carefully supervised rotation program.

By Employees

Most of those college-graduate employees interviewed who participated in formal training programs found them valuable. "Loop" courses are believed to be particularly useful in acquainting the trainee with personnel throughout the company, as well as in giving him a bird's-eye view of company operations. The major shortcomings are the unevenness of instruction from department to department and a tendency to give too much emphasis to procedural detail.

The case method is preferred to straight lectures in classroom training. Branch office training is found helpful for the home office employee if his position involves contact with the field, but it does not provide much familiarity with home office operations. Some of the employees who were assigned to permanent positions without formal training received excellent on-the-job coaching, and are inclined to consider preliminary training as a waste of time unless their work necessitates considerable interdepartmental contact. Others of this group are disappointed by the quality of the on-the-job training they received.

GROUP SALES AND SERVICE

Half the companies polled which sell group insurance have instituted formal training programs for group sales and service representatives. These programs devote a greater proportion of training time to classroom instruction than the programs for strictly home office positions. This instruction is followed by on-the-job training in a branch office. One company maintains a four-week program; the programs of several companies run for two to three months; and another company exposes the trainees to home office operations for one or two years before they are sent into the field. Usually a trainee works in the servicing phases of group insurance first, and after he gains experience and maturity he may move into sales work.

PROGRAMS FOR WOMEN

In seven companies, women are occasionally included in formal training programs designed for male college graduates. Frequently these are women with several years service; seldom are they recent graduates. At least two companies have embarked on more or less extensive formal programs for new female college graduates. The actuarial department of one large company hires female mathematics majors from colleges in the vicinity of the home office for training leading to moderately high-level technical positions within the actuarial department. A multiple-line company is willing to hire women who plan to be with the company at least one year, and offers them training varying in duration from three months to two years. College women are recruited for work of different degrees of complexity in the casualty underwriting, group underwriting, and actuary departments.

SUMMER TRAINING

Several companies have introduced summer training programs for college students in order to acquaint them before graduation with employment opportunities available in the home office and to be able to observe them at work prior to hiring them for permanent employment. Actuarial departments frequently hire mathematics majors for summer training between their junior and senior years in college. A large company recently announced the inauguration of an internship program in its controller's department. Accounting majors from colleges of business administration are to be selected for several months' work with the company during part of their senior year. This internship program is similar to those established by several large public-accounting firms.

HUMAN RELATIONS PROBLEMS

Executives of companies in which formal training programs have been in operation over a period of years find that the human relations problems they provoke seldom are particularly serious. Most companies allow qualified non-college personnel to enter the college training program. In actuality, a relatively small number of non-college employees have been admitted to these programs; if a regular employee possesses outstanding capacity, he will generally have advanced too far with the company to be willing to begin all over again as a trainee. Most personnel directors favor frank discussions of the training program with groups of non-college supervisors. Admission to the training program, it is emphasized, is no guaranty of promotion, although the odds are in favor of the capable trainee. The non-college employees are urged to avail themselves of the L.O.M.A. and C.L.U. courses or to continue their higher education at night in order to improve their own chances of promotion.

TRAINEE TURNOVER

Most of the companies which are leaders in the field of college recruitment and training are quite pleased with their ability to retain college graduates after they have trained them. One company reported that 20 out of its 28 trainees of the class of 1948 were still with the company in 1952; of the 1949 class, 17 out of the 28 remained; and of the 1950 class, 13 out of 16. Another company finds that it has retained more than 75 per cent of its college graduates. These figures compared favorably with the results of a survey of a large number of trainees in all branches of business; that survey revealed a first year separation rate of 42 per cent.

g. AFTER TRAINING

PLACEMENT OF TRAINEES

When Decided

After training the college-level employee, those companies with well-organized programs give careful consideration to his proper assignment as a productive member of the home office organization. Where the training involves exposure to a variety of company operations, one might expect placement decisions to be made after the trainee has gained experience in the different departments and has discovered where his interests and aptitudes lie. But only one third of the companies with formal training programs decide on placement at the end of the training period; another third of these companies determine permanent assignments during training; and the remaining third, before training begins.

Line *vs.* Staff

Where the college program is firmly established in the company, either because it has been in existence for a long time or because it enjoys wholehearted top-management support, graduates of the program are placed in all parts of the organization, in both line and staff functions. In other companies, most college trainees, as well as college graduates who are assigned to positions without a preliminary general training program, are assigned to staff positions almost exclusively. It is considered safer to place them in specialized positions to which the non-college employees do not aspire.

Reception by Supervisors

Supervisory personnel who have attained their positions after many years of line work without the benefit of a college education do not, on the whole, exhibit hostility toward graduates of the training program. The reception given the trainee by the supervisor varies with the individual personalities involved. In many cases, the supervisors are quite enthusiastic; only occasionally do they accept the training program graduate with hesitation.

Ease of Placement Affected by:

Company Growth

Two factors which either magnify or reduce the problems involved in placing the college graduate are the growth of the company and the importance of seniority in promotion policy. Some company officials report that friction resulting from the placement of college trainees does not arise because the company is growing so fast and in so many directions that there are more vacancies than there are qualified individuals to fill them.

Importance of Seniority

Where it is the company's express policy to promote on the basis of ability without regard to seniority, no problem arises when a training program graduate with relatively brief service is placed in a position for which experienced employees are also being considered, if it can be demonstrated that the younger man is best fitted for the job.

Follow-up

Personnel and training people in companies with well-established training programs for college graduates make a special effort to watch over their ex-trainees lest they get "lost" in the organization or "stuck in a rut." Usually they keep up-to-date records of the present position and performance of each training program graduate, and are consulted by line management when vacancies occur.

MANAGEMENT DEVELOPMENT PROGRAMS

Company officials who are familiar with these activities in other branches of industry are convinced that life insurance home offices should institute long-range programs of management development which will prepare college trainees, as well as other employees of promise, for top-level positions. Few, if any, life insurance companies have established comprehensive management development programs, but they do engage in activities which encourage the development of executive talent.

A management development program suitable for the life insurance home office was outlined before the Life Office Management Association in 1947. The program, which is typical of similar activities in other industries, contains five elements:

1. Organization planning to determine the company's present and future executive needs.

2. Analyzing the requirements of each key position.

3. Appraising executives to identify those with the greatest promotion potential and to determine their training needs.

4. Inventorying the availability and ready status of potential replacements.

5. Planning development programs to meet company and individual needs.[1]

Organization Planning

Officer Appraisal

Personnel Inventory

Only 7 of the 65 companies polled indicated that they had undertaken formal organization planning to determine their present and future executive needs. Six have embarked on a program of appraising junior executives, and 2 more were contemplating this activity in 1952. Personnel officials interviewed were hesitant about suggesting an appraisal program involving senior, as well as junior, officers. Twelve of the life companies maintain some kind of personnel inventory system, with 4 more planning one for the future.

1. Ewing W. Reilley, "More Effective Management Through Executive Development," *Proceedings of the 1947 Annual Conference, Life Office Management Association* (New York: L.O.M.A., 1948), p. 13.

Supervisory Training

About one-third of the companies polled have instituted a series of lectures or conferences for lower-level supervisory personnel. In addition to classes preparing for the L.O.M.A. examination found in a large number of home offices, ten companies have adopted the wartime Training Within Industry courses. These consist of conferences to develop skill in leading (Job Relations Training,) skill in planning (Job Methods Training,) and skill in instructing (Job Instruction Training.) A substantial number of companies have developed their own programs in the middle management area. These programs may include the TWI courses or their equivalent, and then continue at a somewhat more sophisticated level. At least one company conducts a seminar for top management. Under the guidance of a professor of business administration, this company's executives discuss cases involving human relations in business.

Job Rotation

An important aspect of management development in many firms outside the life insurance industry is a planned program of job rotation. Thirteen of the life companies polled reported some interdepartmental job rotation above the trainee level. None of the officers queried is of the opinion that interdepartmental job rotation is feasible on the senior officer level, but many feel it can be accomplished successfully among junior officers and supervisors.

Committee Assignments

Most life insurance companies make more or less extensive use of interdepartmental committees to decide matters affecting the company as a whole. While few of the companies consciously make use of committee assignments to develop management material, executives report that their department heads are becoming more "company-minded" and somewhat less "department-minded" as a result of committee assignments which allow for interdepartmental exchange of views.

Multiple Management

Seven life insurance companies report that they have established "multiple management" plans under which representatives of middle management are appointed to a junior board of directors or the equivalent, with power to submit recommendations to the board of directors or to top management.

Other Devices

Other devices which life insurance companies employ in developing managerial talent include "assistant-to" and other staff assignments, observational tours within the company and in other companies, and attendance at professional conferences sponsored by such organizations as the American Life Convention, the Life Insurance Agency Management Association, and the Life Office Management Association. Several of the larger companies have sent officers to management training courses given by universities, the best known of which is the Advanced Management Program at Harvard. A seminar in life insurance management problems, instituted at Columbia in 1951, has been attended by representatives of leading life insurance companies in the New York City area.

Top-Management Support

Because technical specialists, rather than experts in administration *per se,* occupy the top positions of most life insurance companies, it is sometimes difficult for personnel people to convince top management of the necessity for a management development program. But there is general agreement that such programs must be enthusiastically supported by top management if they are to be successful.

2. RECOMMENDATIONS

Most of the recommendations which follow are based upon suggestions made by people in the life insurance industry or upon activities currently pursued in some companies. It is recognized that many of them are inapplicable to a given home office situation. These recommendations are presented in the hope that they may inspire management to develop better ones.

COLLEGE RECRUITING FOR MANAGEMENT RESERVOIR

Company management should plan now for the eventual replacement of junior and senior officers, as they retire, by relatively young, vigorous, and competent persons who have grown up with the company. The practice of bringing in such individuals from the outside when they are needed is destructive to morale. Frequently the right man is difficult to find, or can be enticed away from his current connection only at a high price. *It makes more sense actively to recruit college graduates at the trainee level and develop them for future management responsibility.* The human-relations problems which this practice may raise have not been found to be of great magnitude by companies with much experience in college recruiting.

This is intended to imply, not that four years in college automatically equips an individual to shoulder important responsibilities, but rather that the probability of finding officer material among college graduates is greater than among the population as a whole because able and intelligent high school graduates today generally make every effort to obtain a higher education. Life insurance companies should not, however, discriminate against applicants for employment without college degrees if those applicants seem to possess other desirable qualifications. Such individuals should be encouraged to continue their education by correspondence or class attendance at night.

Stimulating Work

If a company decides to hire sufficient college-level manpower to provide a reservoir of future management material, *its major problem will be to provide work sufficiently stimulating to keep these employees contented until they are ready for managerial responsibility and until such positions are available.* This problem is magnified because much of home office operations involves clerical routine. *It may be faced by hiring only those who can tolerate a minimum of such routine.* The extremely ambitious, extroverted "salesman type" should be encouraged to go into life insurance sales, perhaps eventually to return to the home office in the agency department after a successful career in personal production.

Planned Job Rotation

Planned job rotation is valuable in preventing the employee from being overwhelmed by the routine nature of a job. It takes a number of months to become thoroughly familiar with a given task and during this time it will not be considered routine. *These employees should be encouraged, if not expected, to continue their education in insurance and related lines after employment.* The requirement of a Fellowship in the Life Office Management Association Institute and of the Chartered Life Underwriter designation will not only give the individual a well-rounded background in insurance, but will provide the challenge lacking in a routine position.

Continued Education

Tangible rewards should be offered for each examination passed and study allowed on company time.

Top-Management Support

From the writer's observation and from the testimony of many closely connected with the industry, *the most important factor which will keep high-grade individuals content to wait until they are ready for managerial responsibility is a knowledge that top management is genuinely interested in their progress and intends to place them in positions of responsibility when the openings occur.* One company has a truly outstanding training program in the opinion of a substantial number of its graduates who were interviewed, but in the six years that the program has been in operation, the company has lost about two-thirds of its trainees. The main reason appears to be that its top management recognizes the need for these trainees only in highly specialized and restricted positions. They are kept in one division of the company and are looked upon with some skepticism by the rest of the organization.

Continual Supervision

The intelligent college graduate does not require a written guarantee that he will be a department manager in five years and an officer in ten. *He wants, rather, assurance that his work is being observed, appreciated, and criticized when necessary.* A frequent complaint from the employees interviewed is that they are never told when they do a bad job. *It might be appropriate not only for the individual's immediate superior and department head to keep track of his progress, but for the official in charge of college recruiting and training also to review his work periodically and to apprise him of his strengths and weaknesses.* This official should also be consulted when openings develop throughout the company so that he may make recommendations, where appropriate, from his roster of college-level employees; and, ideally, he should be part of a high-level committee supervising the rotation of promising employees from job to job to get company-wide experience. Such employees should be made to feel that their chances of promotion are being enhanced, rather than jeopardized, by the rotation; otherwise they will probably prefer to build their careers in one department where they are known and appreciated by their superiors and subordinates. Here they become experts in only one phase of the business and will be less likely to acquire sufficient background for top management positions.

SUFFICIENT STARTING SALARIES TO ATTRACT MARRIED MEN

Life insurance companies would do well to pay starting salaries which will attract college graduates who are already married or expect to be in the near future, since such individuals find the security of home office employment more important than do unmarried young people. If lower turnover should result from this policy, the savings therefrom will more than compensate for the higher salaries paid. A return to "normal" levels of business activity should bring an end to the highly inflated starting salaries offered by industrial firms, and insurance salaries will cease to be so far outclassed.

CENTRALIZED RECRUITING RESPONSIBILITY

If a company determines actively to recruit college graduates for home office employment, it should centralize the responsibility for the entire program. The individual or department given this responsibility should maintain continuous contact with the placement directors of a limited number of institutions in the area if the company's needs are small; or in the case of large organizations, these contacts should be on a regional or nationwide basis. *Campus visits, rather than mere correspondence, are essential.* Wherever possible, a recent graduate of the college visited should accompany the recruiter to provide a personal link between the campus and the company. If sales personnel are recruited in colleges, it may be desirable for a representative of the field force to visit the campus at the same time. Although the home office representative recruits for sales as well as non-sales positions in the life companies with the most highly regarded college programs, it is probably undesirable for a sales representative to recruit for home office positions as well as for sales. A dedicated and successful salesman cannot help presenting non-sales work as a poor second choice to a career in sales. No more than two company representatives should interview a candidate at the same time, however, lest he feel intimidated by the prospect of "going before a board."

Campus Visits

Recruiting by Sales Personnel

HOME OFFICE VISITS

Promising applicants should be invited to the home office at company expense for interviews with personnel people, department heads, and at least one senior officer. They should also have the opportunity to meet informally with recent employees from the same school or at least from the same region of the country. If considerable weight is given to aptitude, mental level, or interest tests, some of this testing might be done on campus to reduce the number invited to the home office. Every effort should be made to notify successful and unsuccessful candidates as soon as possible. Several questionnaire respondents reported that they took other employment when they were kept "dangling" too long by a life insurance company.

RECRUITING LITERATURE

In view of the general ignorance of home office employment opportunities which obtains on most campuses today, the life insurance companies should be far more vigorous in providing literature designed to inform undergraduates of these opportunities. In addition to elaborately printed brochures made available for placement office libraries, the life companies should distribute brief, inexpensive pamphlets or even mimeographed sheets indicating the employment opportunities, qualifications desired, and salaries currently offered, in sufficient quantity so that interested students may take them from the placement office. Literature should contain detailed information on the training and positions offered, and indicate the paths of progress available to the college-graduate employee. The careers of representative employees might be traced to give concrete evidence of the advancement opportunities available.

Brief Pamphlets

Informing Insurance Teachers

Literature on home office opportunities should be provided to teachers of insurance as well as to placement directors. The chapter on home office organization found in most insurance texts lends itself to a discussion of employment opportunities for college graduates that the writer has found to be well-received by his students. Insurance teachers may prefer to allow home office representatives to tell about these opportunities themselves during a class period.

ACADEMIC STANDING OF RECRUITS

Successful home office employees may be obtained, in this writer's opinion, from all ranks of a graduating class. Life companies should strive to obtain their share of the very top individuals from which, it is to be expected, future presidents and vice-presidents will be secured; but there are many lesser managerial positions in which the "average" graduate may find his niche. Evidence of ability to work harmoniously with others should, however, be required of all such persons hired.

FORMAL TRAINING PROGRAMS

There is no doubt that some sort of formal training program should be offered by any company that is seriously interested in attracting college graduates. The nature of this training will naturally vary from company to company. As a result of considerable discussion with those in charge of a variety of training programs and with a large number of employees who have gone through them, the following program is suggested:

Suggested Program:

The initial training period should take the form of *a rather elaborate orientation program* to acquaint the new college-level employee with the life insurance industry, the major functions of the company, and its organization; and to give him a bird's-eye view of the operations and personnel of the different departments. *The program might start with a series of introductory lectures geared to the college-level audience and given by someone with experience in addressing such audiences.* While some remarks by the president or other senior executive would be most appropriate, it is probably undesirable to call upon large numbers of operating department officials to come before the group and give detailed explanations of the functions of their departments. A number of employees remarked that too many of these officials emphasize details which are quickly forgotten, or make the "after-dinner" type of speech which their audience tends to dismiss as "propaganda."

Introductory Lectures

Abbreviated "Loop" Course

Acquaintance with personnel throughout the company and with the positions available may be obtained in an abbreviated "loop" course with no more than a few days spent in each department. During each departmental visit, informal conferences should be held with the major officials. The trainees should be, not merely "lectured at," but put to work briefly on the actual operations of the department. Where this is not practical, some kind of "dummy" project may be devised which will give the trainees a notion of the flow of work through the department. The presentations of each department should be observed and coordinated by the individual in charge of the program, in order that they be kept stimulating and effective, and prevented from bogging down in the press of daily business.

Summer Training

It might be profitable to invite groups of college juniors for training in the home office in the summer between their junior and senior years, a currently wide-spread practice for actuarial students. If such a program is developed, these students should not be put to work filing cards or performing other menial tasks, because it is unlikely that many able persons so assigned would return to the company after graduation. Perhaps these summer employees could participate in the orientation program just outlined.

Placement

After this orientation program, which should last a month or six weeks, the college graduate may be given a "permanent" position, assigned in as close accordance to his individual preference as possible. *He should remain under the jurisdiction of the training department for the first two or three years, so that he may be reassigned as necessary for his own benefit and for that of the company.*

Job Rotation

After the individuals have found their niche as permanent employees, those who desire it and who evidence top management potential may be included in the rotation program previously mentioned, under which they will spend a year or two in each of several different divisions of the company.

Except in very large organizations, it is unlikely that formal classroom training is feasible for specific positions which must be learned on the job. "Learning by doing" is probably the best method, provided the trainee has access to intelligent, sympathetic superiors and associates who will do an effective coaching job. For such activity to be most effective, it should be company policy that an individual is not eligible for promotion until he has trained a satisfactory understudy.

COLLEGE RECRUITING AND TRAINING: PART OF MANAGEMENT DEVELOPMENT

The suggestions made for the recruiting and utilization of college graduates are an obvious extension of the management development program described above. Once management plans for its future executive needs and develops an inventory of "the availability and ready status of potential replacements," it will very probably embark upon a college recruitment program, if it has not already done so. The initial training of the college recruits is an important phase of the "development programs to meet company and individual needs." If college graduates are made to feel that they are part of a company-wide management development program, it should not be difficult to attract and retain individuals of the highest caliber.

❋ *Appendices* ❋

⁂ Appendix I ⁂

QUESTIONNAIRE FOR LIFE INSURANCE COMPANY OFFICERS

Please return to: Professor Oscar Harkavy
School of Business Administration
University of North Carolina
Box 190
Chapel Hill, North Carolina

We would appreciate receiving the completed questionnaire on or before 15 October 1952.

I. Company Characteristics

1. Name of company: (Answer optional) 2. Mutual ( ) Stock ( )
3. Location of company: Northeast ( ) Southeast ( ) Middle West ( ) Northwest ( ) Southwest ( )
4. Asset size of company: Under $50 million ( ) $50-100 million ( ) $100-250 million ( ) $250-500 million ( ) $500-1,000 million ( ) Over $1 billion ( )
5. Number of employees in home office: (Please include officers. Exclude printing, building maintenance, lunch room staffs, and field office staffs.)
   Under 100 ( ) 100-250 ( ) 250-500 ( ) 500-1,000 ( ) 1,000-5,000 ( ) Over 5,000 ( )
6. Types of business written: Ordinary ( ) Group ( ) Accident and Health ( ) Industrial ( )
   a. What year did company enter group field?
   b. What year did company enter accident and health field?
7. Approximate percentage change in insurance in force during past ten years:
   Increase: 0-10% ( ) 10-50% ( ) 50-75% ( ) 75-100% ( ) Over 100% ( )
   Decrease: ( )
8. Number of senior officers (department heads and above):
   Number of senior officers who are college graduates:

9. Number of junior officers:
   Number of junior officers who are college graduates:

10. Approximate per cent home office staff college trained: (Please include those with two years of college or more.)
    Male: 0-10% ( ) 10-20% ( ) 20-50% ( ) 50-75% ( ) 75-100% ( )
    Female: 0-5% ( ) 5-10% ( ) Over 10% ( )

II. Company Recruiting Experience

11. Do you feel you are getting a sufficient number of college-trained personnel for your present home-office needs?
    If not, what do you feel are the principal reasons for this?

12. Do you feel you are getting a sufficient number of college-trained personnel for your future needs? (e.g. for eventual replacement of junior and senior officers?)

13. During the past five years, approximately what percentage of new male employees has been college graduates? (Please exclude printing, building maintenance, etc., as well as legal and medical positions.)
    0-10% ( ) 10-25% ( ) 25-50% ( ) 50-75% ( ) 75-90% ( ) 90-100% ( )

14. How would you appraise the typical non-veteran college graduate you have employed in terms of:
    a. Adequacy of college training? (Where do specific deficiencies lie?)
    b. Ability to get along with others?
    c. Attitude toward job responsibilities?
    d. Please comment concerning significant differences in ability and attitude between veteran and non-veteran college graduates you have employed.

15. What are the most serious problems which you have encountered in working with the college graduate after you select and hire him?

16. How would you characterize the attitude toward new college graduates on the part of non-college trained employees?
    a. Recent employees
    b. Employees with several years' service.

17. Did you actively recruit new college graduates prior to 1930 ( ); in 1930-1941 ( ), 1946 ( ), 1947 ( ), 1948-1949 ( ), 1950-1952 ( )?
    Do you plan active recruiting at colleges in 1953?

18. For what home office positions do you customarily recruit new college graduates?
    Actuarial trainee ( ) Underwriter ( ) Claims ( ) Security analyst ( ) Mortgage analyst ( ) Accountant ( ) Personnel ( ) Advertising ( ) Public Relations ( ) Statistics ( ) Methods ( ) Group policyholder service respresentative ( )
    Other Positions:

19. Centralization of recruiting: (Please check appropriate description(s).)
    ( ) 1. No formal plan. Sufficient number of graduates apply directly to meet company's needs.
    ( ) 2. Department heads determine their own needs and sources of new employees. Some may contact colleges, others may not.
    ( ) 3. Branch managers recruit for home office as well as for sales positions.

( ) 4. Recruitment is decentralized, but a central office assists department heads and/or branch managers in contacting colleges.
( ) 5. Formal recruiting program for actuarial trainees only.
( ) 6. Centralized recruitment office contacts colleges to fill home office positions.
( ) 7. Centralized recruitment office contacts colleges to fill both home office and sales positions as well.
( ) 8. Other plan. (Please describe.)

20. Is your contact with college placement officers continuous ( ) or sporadic, as the need arises ( )? By campus visits ( ), correspondence ( ), or both ( )?

21. Please indicate any past experience, favorable or otherwise, you may have had in college recruiting.
    a. Quality of interviewees
    b. Cooperation extended by placement office

22. What changes, if any, in present recruitment practices are contemplated by top management?

23. Does your company issue literature expressly designed for recruiting college graduates for home office positions? (If so, we should greatly appreciate your forwarding a copy to us.)

24. How many colleges do you contact in a typical year?

25. Do you recruit from local colleges only ( ), or on a regional ( ), or national basis ( )?

26. Over the past five years have you hired more graduates of liberal arts colleges ( ) or of colleges of business administration ( )?
    a. For what positions do you prefer liberal arts training?
    b. For what positions do you prefer undergraduate business administration training?
    c. For what positions do you prefer graduate business administration training?

27. Do you feel the completion, prior to employment, of a college course in life insurance is necessary ( ), highly desirable ( ), desirable ( ), of little importance ( ), undesirable ( )?

28. Do you feel the completion prior to employment, of a college course in general insurance is necessary ( ), highly desirable ( ), desirable ( ), of little importance ( ), undesirable ( )?

29. For what positions, if any, do you require a major in insurance?

30. Do you use newspaper ads ( ), and/or employment agencies ( ) to recruit recent college graduates?

31. Do you obtain most of your actuarial trainees from universities offering actuarial courses ( ), or from liberal arts colleges ( )?

32. a. Have your starting salaries been competitive with those offered by companies seeking the same quality of college-graduate recruits in: 1946-47 ( ), 1948-49 ( ), 1950-52 ( )?
    b. If not competitive, do you feel that you thereby lost one or more good prospective employee(s) you might otherwise have been able to employ?

33. In 1952, what starting monthly salary did you offer:
    a. Inexperienced college graduates without special training?

b. Actuarial trainees, no examinations passed?
c. Actuarial trainees, three examinations passed?
d. Holders of degree of Master of Business Administration?

34. a. What are the principal advantages your company can offer the prospective home office employee?
b. What are the principal disadvantages of employment in the home office?

35. Do you use mental level ( ), aptitude ( ), interest ( ), or personality ( ) tests as an aid in screening new college graduates? If so, please name those you use.
Have you checked their validity in your own company?

36. Have you a formal orientation program for the new employee? If so, please describe briefly.

III. Training

37. Has your company a formal actuarial training program?
If so, what form does this training take?
Number of persons currently in training:

38. Has your company a formal training program (or programs) for non-actuarial home office positions?
If so, please describe, indicating use of job rotation, on-the-job training, classroom instruction, home assignments, etc. Please note length of time spent on each phase.
When was this program instituted?
Number of persons currently in training:
Number of persons trained since beginning of program?

39. a. Has your company a formal training program for group sales and/or service representatives?
If so, please describe.
b. Do you expect group trainees to stay in the group department, or encourage them to enter Ordinary sales?

40. If a formal training program of any kind is not in effect, to what positions are new college graduates initially assigned?

41. Is the institution of a formal program(s) under consideration by top management? What is its attitude toward such programs?

42. Is it company policy to admit other employees to college training programs?
In actuality, have many other employees been admitted?

43. Has your company any formal training program(s) for women?
If so, please describe.
Are women admitted to any of the foregoing programs?

IV. Placement (Relevant only to those companies having formal training programs.)

44. Is placement decided at begining of training ( ), during training ( ), at end of training ( )?

45. Are graduates of college training programs typically placed in line positions ( ), staff positions ( ), or both ( )?

46. Have line supervisors received training program graduates enthusiastically ( ), or with hesitation ( )? Does reaction vary with supervisor?

47. Please indicate typical positions into which non-actuarial, home office training program graduates have been placed.

48. Do non-college employees fear their promotion opportunities are adversely affected by training program graduates?
How have you handled this situation, if it exists or has existed?

V. Turnover

49. Has turnover among college graduates been greater ( ), about the same ( ), or lower ( ) than among non-college male employees?

50. A life insurance company president has been quoted as follows: "Today many of the college graduates are discontented. They want to move along more rapidly than the insurance structure will allow. Their income is not increasing rapidly enough to suit them and their desire is to assume positions of increased responsibility faster than they are ready for them or more rapidly than these positions become available."
Please comment on this statement in the light of your own company's experience.

VI. Salary

51. Please indicate approximate 1952 salary of a college graduate, hired in 1947, who has made average progress with your company.
At what salary did he start in 1947?

VII. Management Development

52. Has your company undertaken formal organization planning to determine its present and future executive needs? If so, please describe procedure.

53. Has your company undertaken a formal program of appraising junior executives to identify those with greatest promotion potential and to determine their training needs?

54. Has your company developed a plan for inventorying the availability and ready status of potential replacements for key positions?

55. Has your company instituted development programs on the management or supervisory level? If so, please describe briefly.

56. What part has top management played in this program?

57. If no such program has been instituted, is one under consideration by top management?

58. Please indicate which, if any, of the following devices are used in your company as a means of developing overall company knowledge on the part of management:
    1. Job rotation or interfunctional training (i.e. rotation without full job responsibility) ( )
    Do you consider interdepartmental job rotation feasible on the senior officer level ( ), junior officer level ( ), supervisory level ( )?

2. Committee assignments ( )
   Is there a plan of rotating committee assignments among officers?
3. Internship (assistant-to positions) ( )
4. "Multiple management" plans ( )
5. Observation tours ( )
6. Formal classes ( )
7. Conferences ( )
8. Understudy positions ( )
9. Other device(s)

59. How important is seniority in your company's policy on promotion?

60. It is widely believed that the salary structure of life insurance companies is materially below that of other industries. In order to determine the truth of this allegation, we should greatly appreciate your completing the following table. *Your company's data will, of course, be kept confidential.* We shall publish summaries only, from which identification of individual company statistics will be impossible. This sheet may be returned separately.

Please fill in the following three lines only if this sheet is sent separately from the rest of the questionnaire:

Mutual ( ) Stock ( )

Location of company: Northeast ( ) Southeast ( ) Middle West ( ) Northwest ( ) Southwest ( )

Asset size of company: Under $50 million ( ) $50-100 million ( ) $100-250 million ( ) $250-500 million ( ) $500-1,000 million ( ) Over $1 billion ( )

Distribution of Salaries

Please indicate the number of MALE employees, having FIVE OR MORE YEARS OF SERVICE, in each salary category

Annual Salary	*Home Office*		*Field*
	Executive, supervisory or technical *	Group Sales & Service	Agency Management Staff
Under $5,000			
$ 5,000 to 5,999			
6,000 to 7,499			
7,500 to 10,000			
10,000 to 15,000			
15,000 to 20,000			
20,000 to 25,000			
25,000 and over			
Total Number			

* Please exclude printing, building maintenance, lunchroom staffs.

Additional remarks and suggestions are welcomed.

✻ *Appendix II* ✻

QUESTIONNAIRE FOR COLLEGE AND UNIVERSITY PLACEMENT DIRECTORS

Please return to: Professor Oscar Harkavy
School of Business Administration
University of North Carolina
Box 190
Chapel Hill, North Carolina

We would appreciate receiving the completed questionnaire on or before 15 October 1952.

1. Name of Placement Director:
   (Answer optional)
2. College or University:
   (Answer optional)
3. Location: New England ( ) Middle Atlantic ( ) Midwest ( ) Northwest ( ) Southeast ( ) Southwest ( )
4. Degrees granted: Liberal Arts ( ) Business Administration, undergrad. ( ) Business Administration, grad. ( )
5. Number of courses offered in General Insurance ( ), in Life Insurance ( ), in Property and Casualty Insurance ( )
6. Is a major in insurance offered?
7. In terms of student body enthusiasm, would you rate the insurance program as outstanding ( ), above average ( ), average ( ), below average ( )?
8. How would you appraise the average student's knowledge of the life insurance industry and home office employment opportunities?
9. How does the life insurance industry rank in popularity with other industries bidding for your graduates?
10. What do you feel are the principal reasons for its popularity or lack thereof?
11. Are property and casualty companies more ( ) or less ( ) popular with students than the life companies? Why is this the case?

12. Is it easier to recruit for life insurance company sales ( ) or non-sales ( ) positions?

13. Do the life insurance companies typically obtain their "share" of top-notch graduates (in terms of leadership, personality, scholarship, etc.) for employment in home offices?

    Are there specific life insurance companies which do?

    How would you account for their success?

14. Are there any personality or scholarship characteristics which typify those who accept employment in life insurance company home offices?

15. Which home office positions seem most attractive? Which least attractive?

16. Do students express strong preference for those life insurance companies which offer a formal training program?

17. What do you regard as the requisites for an optimum training program?

18. Do you feel branch managers may successfully recruit for home office positions?

19. Do you feel home office representatives should recruit for both home office and sales positions?

20. Approximately how many life insurance companies visit your office or contact you sporadically to fill occasional vacancies?

21. Approximately how many life insurance companies visit your office on an annual (or semi-annual) basis for home office recruitment?

22. Approximately how many property and casualty company representatives visit your office on an annual (or semi-annual) basis for home office recruiting?

23. How would you appraise the caliber of life insurance company recruiters?

24. Would you care to describe any outstandingly good or bad examples of life insurance company recruiting technique for home office positions?

25. How would you appraise the literature specifically designed for home office recruitment which the life insurance companies make available?

26. Please indicate if starting salaries offered to non-technical graduates in the following positions are typically below, above, or equal to the starting salaries offered by life insurance companies for home office positions.

	Above	Below Life Insurance	Equal to
Accounting, public	( )	( )	( )
Accounting, industrial	( )	( )	( )
Advertising	( )	( )	( )
Banking	( )	( )	( )
Sales, tangible	( )	( )	( )
Sales, intangible	( )	( )	( )
Production management	( )	( )	( )
Retailing	( )	( )	( )
Utilities	( )	( )	( )

27. We should appreciate your supplying as many of the following data as are readily available:

	Class of 1950	*Class of 1951*	*Class of 1952*
Number of graduating seniors:			
Number placed by placement office:			
Number placed in insurance (all phases):			
Number placed in life insurance:			
Number placed in life insurance, non-sales:			
Number placed in life insurance, sales:			

28. Has the number of graduates placed in life insurance company home offices returning to the placement office for aid in obtaining a new position been higher ( ), about the same ( ), or lower ( ) than for graduates placed in other fields?

29. Have graduates placed in life insurance company home offices expressed any significant criticism of the induction and training process to which they have been subjected?

30. Are there other aspects of life insurance company home office employment with which they have been favorably or unfavorably impressed?

Additional comments are welcomed.

❋ *Appendix III* ❋

QUESTIONNAIRE FOR RECENT COLLEGE GRADUATES WHO REJECTED HOME OFFICE EMPLOYMENT

Please return as soon as possible in the enclosed envelope to:
Professor Oscar Harkavy
School of Business Administration
University of North Carolina
Box 190
Chapel Hill, North Carolina

1. College or university attended by respondent:
2. Respondent is: Male ( ) Female ( ) (Please check)
3. Major field: Degree awarded:
4. Name of life insurance company (ies) with which you declined employment:
5. Starting salary offered you by life insurance company (ies):
6. Name of company with which you accepted employment:
7. Starting salary offered you by company with which you accepted employment:
8. How many other offers of employment did you reject in order to take our present position?

   Names of other companies whose employment offers you declined:
9. Are you at present enrolled in a formal training program conducted for new college graduates?

   If so, we should appreciate your describing this program briefly. (Please indicate the subjects covered; the use made of on-the-job training, job rotation, classroom instruction; as well as other significant aspects of the program.)

   How long do you expect the formal program to last?

   What features of the program seem superior to those contained in the training program offered you by the life insurance company(ies)?
10. Have you been placed in a specific position without first undertaking a formal training program?

    If so, please describe the nature of your duties.

11. Please indicate the critical factors which made you decide against a career in a life insurance company home office. (The following items are offered as suggestions only; we should appreciate your comments on them as well as on factors not mentioned.)
    Starting salary
    Opportunities for advancement in salary
    Opportunities for advancement in responsibility
    Nature of the work
    Growth prospects of the firm
    Growth prospects of the industry
    Location
    Size of firm
    Others:

* *Appendix IV* *

QUESTIONS FOR COLLEGE GRADUATES WHO ACCEPTED HOME OFFICE POSITIONS

1. How would you characterize the attitudes toward you and other college graduates on the part of officers, supervisors, other employees?

2. What are the principal areas of deficiency in your college training?

3. What is the nature of your present job and others you have held since joining the company?

4. How do you appraise your prospects for advancement? How important is seniority in advancement?

5. Are you glad you chose the life insurance home office rather than other employment? How did you happen to go to work for an insurance company? Would you leave for another job at the same salary?

6. Are your present salary and prospects for salary advancement satisfactory?

7. How do the growth prospects of your company affect your future?

8. Would you rather work in a larger or in a smaller organization? Are you satisfied with your working conditions?

9. How do you feel about the security of your position? How important is security to you?

10. Have you any suggestions about the way your company goes about recruiting college graduates?

11. If you were responsible for selecting new college-level employees for your company, what special qualities would you look for?

12. Describe the training you received. What are its strong points? Any suggestions for its improvement?

13. Describe any activities designed to develop you for positions of greater responsibility. Formal management development program? Coaching by supervisor?

14. How do you feel about the prestige associated with life insurance company home office employment?

* Appendix V *

The contribution to this study by the following organizations is gratefully acknowledged:

LIFE INSURANCE COMPANIES

American Mutual Life Insurance Company
American Reserve Life Insurance Company
Atlantic Life Insurance Company
California-Western States Life Insurance Company
Central Life Assurance Company
Colonial Life Insurance Company of America
Commonwealth Life Insurance Company
Connecticut General Life Insurance Company
Connecticut Mutual Life Insurance Company
Equitable Life Assurance Society of the United States
Equitable Life Insurance Company of Iowa
Farm Bureau Life Insurance Company
General American Life Insurance Company
Great American Reserve Insurance Company
Great Southern Life Insurance Company
Guardian Life Insurance Company of America
Home Life Insurance Company
Iowa Life Insurance Company
Jefferson Standard Life Insurance Company
John Hancock Mutual Life Insurance Company
Kansas City Life Insurance Company
Life Insurance Company of Georgia
Life Insurance Company of Virginia
Massachusetts Mutual Life Insurance Company
Metropolitan Life Insurance Company
Midland Mutual Life Insurance Company
Mutual Benefit Life Insurance Company
Mutual Life Insurance Company of New York
National Life and Accident Insurance Company
New England Mutual Life Insurance Company
New York Life Insurance Company
North American Life and Casualty Company
North Carolina Mutual Life Insurance Company
Northern Life Insurance Company

Northwestern Mutual Life Insurance Company
Occidental Life Insurance Company of California
Old American Life Company
Pacific Mutual Life Insurance Company
Penn Mutual Life Insurance Company
Phoenix Mutual Life Insurance Company
Pilot Life Insurance Company
Pioneer Mutual Life Insurance Company
Provident Life and Accident Insurance Company
Provident Mutual Life Insurance Company
Prudential Insurance Company of America
Rio Grande National Life Insurance Company
Shenandoah Life Insurance Company
Southland Life Insurance Company
Southwestern Life Insurance Company
Standard Insurance Company
State Capital Life Insurance Company
State Farm Life Insurance Company
State Mutual Life Assurance Company
Teachers Insurance and Annuity Association
Travelers Insurance Company
Volunteer State Life Insurance Company
Western Life Insurance Company
Wisconsin National Life Insurance Company
Woodmen Accident and Associated Companies

FIRE AND CASUALTY COMPANIES

Insurance Company of North America Companies
Providence Washington Insurance Company
Royal-Liverpool Insurance Group

COLLEGES AND UNIVERSITIES

American University
Baylor University
Boston University
Bowdoin College
Bradley University
Carleton College
Colgate University
College of William and Mary
Columbia University
Cornell University
Dartmouth College
Denison University
De Paul University
Duke University
Emory University
Florida State University
George Washington University
Georgia Institute of Technology
Grinnell College
Harvard University

Johns Hopkins University
Lafayette College
Lehigh University
Michigan State College
New York University
Oberlin College
Occidental College
Ohio State University
Pennsylvania State College
Princeton University
Rutgers University
State College of Washington
Syracuse University
Temple University
Trinity College
Union College
University of Arkansas
University of California, Berkeley
University of California, Los Angeles
University of Chicago
University of Colorado
University of Florida
University of Illinois
University of Kansas
University of Maryland
University of New Mexico
University of North Carolina
University of Notre Dame
University of Oklahoma
University of Oregon
University of Pennsylvania
University of Pittsburgh
University of South Carolina
University of South Dakota
University of Texas
University of Washington
Vanderbilt University
Washington University
Williams College
Yale University

www.ingramcontent.com/pod-product-compliance
Lightning Source LLC
LaVergne TN
LVHW090321210926
848480LV00001B/314
* 9 7 8 0 8 0 7 8 7 9 9 5 5 *